108 Ways
to Market Your Practice

THEODORE W. ROBINSON

INNER HEALING PRESS

108 Ways to Market Your Practice

ISBN 978-0-9786541-2-2

An Inner Healing Press Publication
www.innerhealingpress.com
www.centerforinnerhealing.com

Acknowledgments

First, thank you to my wife, Maria, for her support and love and for accepting my absence from our family while I was writing. She is a wonderful healing partner and is constantly offering support, knowledge and her gentle love in all things.

Next, thank you to Theresa Rodriguez, who edited this book and played an integral role in the cover design. She is also my paralegal and primary assistant in everything in my office. Without her, this book would never have been completed. She is exceptional in every sense of the word.

Thank you to Janine Melillo who has acted as a text editor. Her sage advice and intelligent point of view has been a constant help and her energetic responses have been a constant source of encouragement.

Thank you to my spiritual teachers, Leonard Jacobson and Walter Belling, who have offered their support in so many ways over the years. They have been central to my own internal growth over the years which gave me the strength and drive to write this book.

I also thank Gary Craig for developing Emotional Freedom Technique since it has occupied a central position of importance in my life since I learned it ten years ago. I believe that EFT is offering a fundamental shift in all health care and so many other aspects of life that it will become a mainstay of all personal growth work in the future. It certainly helps eliminate self-limiting factors in people's lives and has helped me personally many times.

Thank you to all those who have read my previous book and offered their sincere expressions of approval and support. Now that you've opened your practices, here is the next step for you to take to achieve success in them and abundance in your lives.

Table of Contents

INTRODUCTION

This book is the second in a series of books intended to assist alternative health care practitioners become full fledged professionals in every sense of the word and also achieve success in your practices. It has been my observation, as a practicing attorney for more than three decades, that many alternative health care practitioners lack a certain professionalism which, if improved upon, would make a big difference in the public's perception of them. That was why I wrote my first book, <u>How to Open or Improve a Successful Alternative Health Care Practice</u>. It is my position that if they look, sound and act like professionals, those who haven't yet sought out their alternative care would more readily do so and that, in turn, would help heal more of the world more effectively.

This second book is intended to assist alternative health care practitioners expand their practices through marketing and to bring their gift of healing to more people. It is a practical book that is meant to demonstrate that marketing one's practice is not only a necessity, but also a good thing to do for the public's sake. If they don't know you exist or know how you can help them, they won't know who you are or how to find you to gain some relief. Marketing is a means to educate and inspire the public to seek you out and make use of your talents as a practitioner.

The techniques offered in this book are practical and will give you the ability to let people know about you and give them a reason to visit you - soon! Of course, once they visit you or your website, it's up to you to give them a good reason to return. The best reason for them to return is because they're satisfied with your services or products. If you give them relief from their pains and discomforts, you are certain to hear from them the next time something similar happens to them. After that, word of mouth will be your greatest asset. However, when that doesn't do the trick, the techniques outlined in this book will help pick up the slack and maintain a steady flow of clients to your office.

In this book, you will also find a means of eliminating any resistance you may feel within yourself to using marketing in your practice. I've been effectively using Emotional Freedom Technique (EFT) in my practices for ten years and I have found that it is the most successful way of eliminating blockages to success and abundance. Whatever it is that holds you back from success can be easily addressed and eliminated in short order using EFT. There is an EFT section in the book that will offer you practical assistance in becoming successful. And, while EFT may look a little silly when you first use it, the technique works and that's all that counts to me. I trust you'll feel the same the first time you achieve success with it. It can be an amazing experience when, out of nowhere, you find yourself feeling better about something that you never thought would ever change in your life.

The rest of the book is dedicated to providing you with the very best information and techniques available today to bring about change in your practice and ultimately success. Use every one of them or use one technique a week, but use them. You can't go wrong. Most of them won't cost you much to do and they will generate new clients for your practice. Of course, once you get new clients into your office, you must "deliver the goods" and offer them relief from whatever ails them. Make sure you keep up-to-date with everything you do and do the best job you can for them and you'll see an almost immediate improvement in your practice. Good luck.

MARKETING YOUR PRACTICE

Many practitioners who enter various alternative and holistic fields do so primarily to help others. They don't really want to spend much time on marketing themselves or their practices. Most feel that their work will speak for itself and draw new clients to them through word of mouth. Many may actually resent the idea that they have to take any of their precious time away from their healing practice to promote it.

However, many soon discover that their practices have barely started before they need to attract more people to them. Some might even lose their practice because they can't get enough clients for their business to survive. This often leads many practitioners to become disappointed and disenchanted. Disappointment can turn into resentment and that can lead to depression and the urge to give up altogether. Not a pretty picture when all they wanted to do was help others heal in some way. So what's the answer?

The reality of business (and yes, even a holistic practice is a business) is that marketing is an absolute necessity in every practice, whether it's an alternative or a mainstream health care practice. However, the approach to take is to recognize that you are bringing your gift of healing to people who might not otherwise discover you. Marketing will give people a chance to find out how you can help them. If they never hear about you or what you do, or worse, can't find you, then they won't benefit from your work. Resolve this basic issue for yourself - that spreading the word and marketing yourself is an important aspect of your practice and it will be for the <u>entire</u> duration of your practice.

Please Note: If you felt any resentment or resistance arising within you when you read that last paragraph, then you probably want to address that resistance first, before you do anything else. Otherwise, you can read everything in this book, digest it and implement it and still nothing will happen! That's the way the Law of Attraction works. If you don't clear the underlying resistance to abundance and success all your efforts could amount to nothing.

You can eliminate the resistance and resentment easily by using Emotional Freedom Technique (EFT). If you're not already familiar with it, EFT is a meridian-based acupressure technique coupled with focused attention. When the two are used together, the technique is amazingly effective. It consists of light tapping on certain specified points around the face and upper body which eliminate blockages within your meridian system that can otherwise cause negative thoughts and self-limiting beliefs to arise within you. Once the blockages are eliminated by tapping on those access points, the negative and self-limiting thoughts are also eliminated in short order. If this sounds too simple, rest assured it's not. It actually works and it works well. I've been an EFT practitioner for ten years and have had success using EFT for just this purpose. Take a look at the Appendix on p. 192 in which EFT is fully explained and shown to you. There are also a number of specific wordings provided for you to follow.

There is also a detailed discussion on p. 215 how to eliminate resistance to abundance and success and any resentment that may exist. This is an important first step that you don't want to pass up. It will set the tone to make everything else you do successful.

- ## Why Should You Market Your Practice in the First Place?

Most alternative health care practitioners don't want to spend any time marketing their practice because they honestly believe it won't be necessary and they simply don't want to do it. It actually grates on many practitioners' minds that they should even take part in any kind of commercial marketing.

They often believe that marketing is nothing more than crass commercialization and they want no part of it. On the other hand, many times practitioners open their doors to offer their services to the public and only a few like-minded people show up. Before long, they find they can't meet their bills and they often lose their initial enthusiasm for their practice. That can, and often does, lead to them leaving their practice and the community loses a great asset, all because of a self-limiting belief that marketing your service is inherently wrong or a bad thing to do. I strongly disagree. I believe marketing is an integral aspect of being in any type of practice.

By marketing your practice, you're letting your community know about the valuable services you are offering them and you are establishing credibility in your name, expertise and reputation. You are also building your practice's "name brand" recognition while bringing new clients into your practice. This is important because when people see your name, you want them to identify it with something positive and helpful to them.

Remember, in all marketing, the important question to keep in mind is, "what's in it for me?" The prospective client/customer/patient always wants to know the answer to that question and when you can answer it positively for them and show them they need what you're offering, they'll beat a path to your door.

There are many ways you can market your practice, but it always comes down to the same question: <u>What are **you** willing to do?</u> If you're not willing to do a particular technique, then don't bother considering it. It will just be a waste of your time. On the other hand, different types of marketing will appeal to different practitioners. This book describes a vast array of unique ways to market your practice. Many are likely to meet your needs.

It's up to you to choose the ones that most appeal to you. Shortly, you'll learn how to use this book to greatest advantage, however, there are a few things you should consider before even looking at the different ways to market your practice. First, determine what your Unique Selling Proposition is and how to most effectively charge for your services. Then, take a look at what you can do to eliminate any mindset that keeps you from being a success. You'll learn how to change that mind-set by using EFT which will allow you to follow through on your new marketing plans.

- **Unique Selling Proposition**

The first thing to do when considering any marketing strategy for your practice is to determine your unique selling proposition (USP). Your USP is what is different, outstanding and unique about your practice that makes your practice stand out and which will draw people to it. It must also convey what unique benefits you provide to your clients and describe how you do it clearly and specifically.

To determine your USP, make a list of all the benefits you offer in your practice, then decide which ones are the most compelling and make those the primary focus of your marketing. Again, if you notice that some resistance comes up, use EFT to eliminate the blockages that prevent you from acknowledging what makes you special, outstanding and unique.

Initially, you'll want to define your USP in about two to three sentences setting forth exactly what you do and how you do it differently than anyone else. What you bring to your clients and how your unique history makes a real difference. Then you'll want to distill those two to three sentences down to a few short words or a phrase. It's important to keep your final USP as short and powerful as you can possibly make it. Otherwise, people will get lost in what you're trying to convey to them. It should sound something like a motto or a catch phrase because that's how people will remember it and you.

Many larger corporations use mottos and catch phrases to contribute to their branding campaign. Branding is a way of establishing a "brand name" for oneself. You know, Home Depot has, "You can do it, we can help." Lowes has, "Lets build something together," and McDonalds now has, "I'm lovin' it!" Every large store has such a phrase which people can use to anchor their thoughts back to that chain of stores. It's actually Neuro Linguistic

Programming (NLP) at work, which, by the way, is also incorporated into part of the EFT regimen because it is so effective.

Just because you may not yet be a large chain of offices doesn't mean you can't establish your own USP phraseology. When Network Chiropractic, now Network Spinal Analysis, first came into being, they established a phrase that set the tone for their entire following. "Changing the World, a Spine at a Time" was a great phrase that worked to keep their intent in everyone's mind. Whenever they saw a T-shirt, a hat or anything else with those words on it, they knew what it was about. It also conveyed a larger purpose which is what you want to remember when establishing your own USP. Some might call it a motto, but it can also be viewed as a USP.

You can establish your own USP and transform it into a simple phrase that works for you and your practice. When we first started our practice, the Center for Inner Healing, we decided we wanted to help the world, but didn't want to take the clients' power away from them by substituting ourselves in the process. We felt that if we did that, we were ultimately disempowering them, instead of empowering them which was our goal. We came up with the motto, "Helping Others Help Themselves," which translated that intent into just four words which was understandable by anyone who read it.

We also set out to literally change the world for the better, so we also added a second motto to our Center. It is "Heal Yourself, Heal the World" which says it again, but in a slightly different way. We were going to go with only one of those two phrases, but felt they both said something slightly different and wanted both of them to be used to describe our practice. The second phrase is intended to be used later in our development when we start to reach a much larger audience - worldwide. The first phrase will nonetheless be maintained throughout our tenure as a healing practice.

If you want to establish your practice at a certain level such as statewide, national or international, it is best to determine that well in advance. By making that decision, you are effectively setting the stage for your long term purpose and intent. When you make that inner choice to do something and relinquish it to your subconscious mind, your subconscious will take it and run with it until it has been accomplished. That is, assuming nothing else lies in the way of taking that direction. If anything does arise that blocks your goal, then it is time to use EFT to clear it. Refer to the EFT section in the Appendix of this book for directions on how to do EFT on this issue.

To summarize, it's best to decide on a Unique Selling Proposition and then boil it down to the fewest words possible while still maintaining the essence of it. That will be the most powerful means of expressing your intentions and goals simultaneously to the world and the world will notice and respond.

• **Setting Goals for You and Your Practice**

Use the list of marketing techniques in the next chapter to set goals for marketing your practice. Notice that they are placed in a fashion to start you and your practice off powerfully right from the start. However, you can change the list any way you want so that it works best for you depending on where you are in the evolution of your practice. Do whatever most appeals to you. It's your list, your goals and your practice, but do something. That's the key.

Next, set a start and a completion date for each method as you prioritize them so they won't just become another marketing idea or concept. That way, you'll make each of them a solid goal that you can seek to achieve at a certain time. Once you've set each goal, do your very best to achieve and monitor each one so you can see the progress you're making. That way, you'll get feedback on how well you're doing at meeting your goals and you'll see much better results in the long run. If you don't set firm goal dates, then the entire thing just becomes another mind game or concept. Concepts rarely get accomplished. That's why you set goals - to achieve them.

It's also a sound idea to set both short and long term goals for your practice. If you're just starting your practice, you may find that it's best to set short term goals to get your practice up and running. Then, as you start to fall into a rhythm or pattern in your practice, it's a good idea to review the results you're getting with your marketing plan every three to six months and, of course, each year.

One thing that most business owners fail to do is make an even longer term plan for themselves and their practices. I suggest that you take a three year and a five year view of where you want your practice to be and write those goals down at the outset. That way, when three and then five years roll around (and they come around much faster than you expect), you'll be able to determine how you've done at accomplishing what you set out to do. You can then adjust your marketing activities accordingly. Make sure to also include in your long term goals any proposed retirement date and/or retirement/pension plans. You'll need to prepare for them well ahead of when you actually need them.

Now, it isn't a do-or-die situation if you don't accomplish the goals you've set out for yourself. They are intended to be guidelines for you so you can keep yourself on track over a period of time. As a professional for more than three decades, I can tell you it is extremely easy to get caught up in whatever you're doing for others and lose yourself in the mix. Many times, I've looked at my desk and wondered how it got that way when I know I'm working hard all the time. But then I realize it looks disorganized because I'm not always paying attention to my needs. I'm too focused on other people's needs. It is an especially easy thing to do for those in the helping fields because there are so many needy people out there seeking your help. That's the last thing you want to do - lose yourself in your work. You must hold your center at all times and keep your feet on the ground or you could get just as lost, just as quickly, as those you're helping.

Again, the best way to do this is by setting goals for yourself and your practice and then monitoring them on a regular basis to see how well it's going. If you're not accomplishing what you wanted, then it's time to change how you do business or change your goals. Whatever you feel most comfortable with is fine, but it is important to know what you're doing and not just get caught up in whatever is happening in your practice at any given time and be dragged along like a small stone in a stream. By monitoring your goals and making changes when necessary, you can retain better control of your practice and your life.

• **Different Ways to Charge for Your Services - Session and Results Achieved vs. Hourly**

There are different ways to charge for your services. Each way carries different benefits and difficulties with it. Some practitioners want to see as many clients as they can because they think that will make them "successful." Others want to earn the most they can from the fewest clients so they have more free time for their personal interests. Whichever way you decide works best for you will help you determine the method you use. Many times your personal goals will dictate how you charge in your practice because you may want more time or more money in your life - or both - and that could be part of your considerations.

Here are a few factors to consider when charging by the session:

First, decide how you wish to define a "session." Once you do that, it will be much easier to figure out how much you want to charge for it. Some practitioners define it as the resolution of whatever particular issue a client came to see them about. Whether it takes ten minutes or an hour to resolve the issue, once it is resolved, the session is completed. Many people like this idea since they'd rather not spend any more time then necessary in a therapist's office.

Next, determine how much you want to charge for each session you do with a client. One way to do it is to check on some of the other practitioners in your area and see how much they're charging. Once you know how much they're charging, you can choose to charge about the same, a little less, or a little more, depending on how good you are at what you do or whether you offer additional services or better outcomes to your clients. The marketplace will decide if you're right in the amount you eventually decide to charge.

If you choose to charge by the hour, then the client should be made aware of that ahead of time and have them agree to it in a signed contract before starting your work. That can be done as part the wording of your intake sheet. Just have them sign it at the end of it. Again, the best way to decide how much you wish to charge by the hour is to check on other practitioners in the area who are doing something similar.

Both of these ways of charging have their limitations. First, there is only so much you can reasonably charge most people. Second, regardless of that, there are only so many hours in the day and days in the week that you can practice. Unless you bring in another practitioner to augment your work, you're limited by the number of hours or sessions you can do. Nonetheless, there are many techniques you can do that will still make you a handsome living by investing a fair amount of time into it. It is explained more fully later in this chapter.

It often makes more sense to charge by the hour. That way, if your client goes over the hour and you have the time to continue working with them, you will get paid for the additional time and attention you give them. This can be a much better approach because it doesn't force you to artificially cut off the session in mid-sentence or mid-thought which often happens when a practitioner has another client coming in at the start of the next hour. Of course, if you're booked every hour on the hour, then it may happen anyway. Make sure you're consistent throughout your practice so none of your clients get wind of different fees for different people. That won't go over well with anyone, except the ones who are enjoying a discount.

The other option is to charge by the session and the results you achieve. For example, Emotional Freedom Technique lends itself to achieving results rapidly. It gets great results and often takes the least time to achieve the results the client wanted from the treatment. This can actually be an excellent Unique Selling Proposition for your practice since many people want to take as little time as possible away from their busy schedules but still want great results. Hence, the modality with the quickest and most effective results can be viewed as being superior and so a premium fee can be charged if agreed upon in advance that may far exceed anything you might earn on an hourly billing basis. More on this later.

• Charging for Your Services on an Hourly or Session Basis

When you charge on an hourly basis, the amount you charge will depend largely upon how much other practitioners (your competition) are charging and what kind of results you can accomplish for your clients. In short, the results you achieve for them can always boost your price above what others are charging once people discover your extraordinary abilities.

If, however, you're not producing extraordinary results, then it's time to do something about the way you practice to change it so you are doing extraordinary work. One thing to do, beyond working on your skills as a practitioner, is to work on is your self-confidence and self-esteem. If you don't see yourself as capable of consistently providing excellent services, then nobody else will either. You can change this by using EFT to eliminate all the self-limiting beliefs in your professional life. Once you eliminate your self-limiting beliefs, you will be amazed at how your professional life and practice will change.

Now, back to the fees issue. If you charge just $100.00 per hour, depending upon where you're located, it can result in quite a handsome income as long as you keep your overhead low and are willing to put the necessary work into attracting clients to your practice and then working your practice effectively.

Here's an example of how the hourly numbers can work:

As a high estimate, if you wanted to work fifty (50) weeks a year and have a gross income (meaning before paying overhead and taxes) of $500,000.00, you'd have to see an average of 100 people each week. That's the number of people you need to actually see and not just schedule because there will be clients who won't or can't show up each week, but that's another issue. To actually see 100 people a week, you'd have to service 20 people a day over a five (5) day work week. That's 20 hours without a break and that would simply be too much to do for a single practitioner.

Now, if you lower your sights a bit to earn a gross income of $150,000.00 per year, that would mean you'd have to see an average of 6 people a day over a five day work week for 50 weeks a year and charge each of them $100. per hour. That may sound a lot more reasonable at first look, but it doesn't take into consideration office overhead (like rent and salaries, etc.) and taxes which may mean it will not be enough income for many people. However, it gives you an idea of how the numbers work so you can figure out how many clients you need to see each day depending upon your hourly charges. If you double the number of people from six to twelve people a day, you'll gross $300,000.00 per year and that would serve anyone quite nicely.

Once you decide how much you want to earn each year and plug in your hourly rate and the number of weeks you want to work, you'll be able to determine the number of people you must see in order to meet your goal. Don't forget that you're always going to need to spend additional time each week at your practice beyond treating clients to do paperwork, keep records and do your billing, to say nothing of instituting the marketing techniques you intend to use.

Charging by the session is about the same thing as hourly, except it may vary depending upon how you define a session. If you say a session is over when you've accomplished the work you set out to do, then it can take as little time as you require to get your work done. In some fields such as hypnosis or EFT, that can take as little as 15 minutes if you're good at what you do. Shortening your sessions can make a huge difference in the amount of time you spend with clients and that allows you additional time to do your office paperwork or marketing that you would otherwise have to do after business hours. Or, it may simply provide you with a little additional free time to enjoy life. No matter what you use your additional time for, it generally means you won't have to work as long as you do when you charge by the hour.

Another benefit to your client of working by the session is they don't have to be in your office as long as on an hourly basis and that means they can go home earlier and have more free time for themselves too. Most people don't want to wait in a waiting room and unless you are working on them and they don't want their treatment to take any longer than absolutely necessary. Charging by the session can be a big benefit for them as well as for you. Of course, this assumes you can deliver the results they want in less than an hour. If it is going to take you longer than a normal session (which is usually 45-60 minutes) to accomplish your work, then it is probably better to charge by the hour so you are assured of being properly compensated for your work.

Whichever way you choose to go with your fee structure, it's imperative that you put everything in writing in advance of starting any treatments so both you and your clients can refer back to those terms and conditions if there's a dispute. Otherwise, there is a much greater likelihood of misunderstandings between you and that's when problems can arise.

- **Charging for Your Services on a Result Basis**

One other way you might consider charging is by the outcome of your work. If a client has a particular goal or outcome in mind, once you help them attain their goal, you get paid a previously agreed upon fee. This works particularly well in areas such as sports where you can be hired to help achieve a particular goal like shaving 5 strokes off someone's golf game or helping a runner push through "the wall" to be able to finish a marathon. Of course, make sure the results you need to help them accomplish is not subjective. The terms should be clearly and unequivocally set forth in a written contract (beyond just an intake sheet that's been signed) so that it is enforceable and both parties are bound by it. Nonetheless, make sure you always get paid beforehand so there is no chance of having to run after your fee after you've helped them achieve their goal.

If you choose to get involved in this area, make sure you delineate in writing exactly what is expected and/or promised in very detailed terms. Proof of success is also a very important aspect that should be included in your contract. For example, if someone wants to improve their golf game and you represent that you can help them by reducing their fears, anxiety, worry, etc. then you must start off with their representation and some sort of proof of their normal golf game.

Say they want to break 90 strokes on a par 4 course, then you should be allowed to see their score card records for the first part of the season or last season to verify their normal range of scores. Then, once you've done your work, you should be given their score cards again and verify they've changed the amount you promised. Once the amount of strokes has been reduced, you are entitled to be paid or release any money you've been holding until you succeeded. And don't be surprised if someone wants you to hold their money in an escrow account until you're finished with your work. They have just as much right to be concerned about paying you in advance of the work being done since a claim such as yours is unusual and may sound outlandish. But, if you can deliver on your promise, then you should get paid.

This very issue once occurred when an inventor went to a toothpaste company and claimed he could double the companies' sales of toothpaste by just changing on thing. Of course, the company wanted to know more about the "invention" before they agreed to the deal. Nonetheless, the "inventor" refused to budge and the company eventually agreed to the contract in writing believing they had nothing to lose. Once the contract was signed the inventor exposed his suggestion that they simply double the size of the toothpaste tube mouth. The company did exactly that and to their delight, their sales doubled, and that's when the trouble started. They refused to pay the man his money. He sued for specific performance on the contract and the Court directed the company to pay him. He had delivered on his promise. The greatest insight from that true story is the lawsuit could have been avoided had the money been paid into an independently held escrow account in advance and released upon the condition that the company's sales doubled. That's why you always want to get paid in advance with this type of contract.

This type of work can apply to baseball pitchers, golfers, bowlers, football players, football kickers, soccer players, basketball players (foul shots in particular), swimmers, Olympians of all sorts, weight lifters, pool players, poker players, physicians, surgeons, lawyers, architects, dentists, public speakers, CEOs, company executives, actors, musicians and a lot more. It can actually apply to almost any participant in any field as long as they can specifically identify what they want to achieve. If you can reduce what they want into a written contract and get paid beforehand or have the money placed in escrow, then this may be the type of contract for you to employ.

Another way to approach this is by using a success bonus or success fee so that when your client achieves that something special that they want because of your efforts, he or she will know it was you that did it and they'll recognize they have to compensate you for your work.

This is a very delicate type of fee structure and should not be used by inexperienced professionals. It is suggested that you get an attorney to draft the contract for you so its well written and binding upon both parties. It should only be used when you can explicitly describe what you're going to do for the client and get them to sign a written contract and pay you in advance. Always make sure the client is comfortable with the entire arrangement or it could go wrong and lead to the loss of a client. However, when you're successful and the client is pleased because you've helped them achieve what they've always dreamed about but never could achieve on their own, it all becomes worthwhile. That's when they are usually willing to pay the bonus you've arranged with them. But beware, some people will renege on this type of deal if the solution to their problem is too simple. They think life has to be more difficult and circuitous.

My general advice is to avoid this type of contract, however, it has been included here for the purpose of offering complete information about fee setting.

HOW TO USE THIS BOOK

On the following pages, you'll find a list of one hundred and eight ways to market your practice for you to consider. This list of titles was included to speed up your review process and to help you better utilize this book. Review the list and choose five (only five) of the marketing techniques you're most willing to do and then give each one a priority number based upon which one most appeals to you. Otherwise, you're likely to get overwhelmed with the entire list and wind up doing none of them. You might also make the mistake of trying to do a lot of them at the same time without succeeding at any of them. Use a pencil because as you go through the list, your initial priorities may change. Make sure you overlay your USP onto each suggestion and see which ones appeal to you the most.

_____ 1. Create a Letter to Your Friends and Family Seeking Referrals (p. 24)

_____ 2. Introductory Letter (p. 26)

_____ 3. Family and Friends Introductory Night (p. 28)

_____ 4. Update Letters (p. 28)

_____ 5. Multiple Letters (p. 30)

_____ 6. A Handwritten Note on Each Letter (p. 31)

_____ 7. Testing Your Letter - What Does That Mean? (p. 34)

_____ 8. Thank You Card Follow-up (p. 35)

_____ 9. Write an Introductory Letter to Professionals for Referrals (p. 36)

_____ 10. Write Holiday and Birthday Cards to Your Clients (p. 39)

_____ 11. Send out a Quarterly Printed Newsletter (p. 40)

_____ 12. Send out a Quarterly Calender of Events to All Practice Members (p. 42)

_____ 13. Make Follow-up Phone Calls to Clients after Treatments (p. 44)

_____ 14. Offer a Free Mini-Session (p. 44)

_____ 15. Conduct an Open House with Free or Reduced Rate Treatments (p. 45)

_____ 16. Teach Your Specialty at Alternative Health Care Organization Conferences (p. 46)

_____ 17. Speak at Local Libraries or Business Groups (p. 48)

_____ 18. Network with Local Businesses at Their Regular Meetings (p. 50)

_____ 19. Join Speakers Groups (p. 51)

_____ 20. Conduct Charitable Holiday Events (p. 52)

_____ 21. Teach a Class at the Local Adult Education (p. 53)

_____ 22. Teach a Class at a Local College (p. 54)

_____ 23. Volunteer Your Time and Talents to Help Indigent People (p. 55)

_____ 24. Hold a Free Screening Day for the Public at Your Office (p. 55)

_____ 25. Sponsor a Little League Team or Other Sports Team (p. 56)

_____ 26. Offer a Free Session to Your Local Church/Temple Leaders (p. 57)

_____ 27. Make Charitable Contributions (p. 58)

_____ 28. Sponsor a Health Fair for the General Public (p. 58)

_____ 29. Offer to Do Introductory Mini-sessions in Other Professional's Offices (p. 60)

_____ 30. Volunteer to Be Part of a Discussion Group or Round Table Symposium (p. 61)

_____ 31. Offer Introductory Educational Meetings for Professionals to Obtain Referrals (p. 62)

_____ 100. Offer Advanced Courses for Qualified Practice Members (p. 176)

_____ 101. Hold Special Events for "Practice Members" Only (p. 177)

    _____ a. Offer a Healing Weekend for Practice Members Only (p. 177)

    _____ b. Offer a Healing Retreat to Practice Members Only (p. 178)

_____ 102. Record and Release CD's about Specific Topics (p. 180)

_____ 103. Prepare and Release a DVD about Something Specific (p. 182)

_____ 104. Become a Member of a Grievance Committee in Your Field (p. 183)

_____ 105. Contact Business Schools to Conduct a Stress Reduction Workshop (p. 184)

_____ 106. Contact Alternative Health Care "Colleges" or Schools to See If You Can Teach or Train Their Students (p. 185)

_____ 107. Obtain Celebrity Testimonials by Offering Free Services (p. 185)

_____ 108. Leave Text or Video Comments on YouTube.com or any Other Website That Accepts Comments (p. 186)

It's now time to go over the specifics of each of the 108 marketing methods to make your practice successful. My suggestion is that you go back to your list and review your priorities. You can then read about each of the extensively described marketing methods that you are interested in.

As you review each method, see how you can apply it to your practice. Watch to see if you have any internal resistance to any of the methods and use the instructions to eliminate that resistance before you start. They work much better when there's no internal resistance holding you back.

MARKETING THROUGH THE MAIL

1.   **Create a Letter to Your Friends and Family Seeking Referrals**

This is the best way to establish a clientele if you are just starting a new practice and to keep it humming whenever your business needs a boost. Just think about it. Nobody wants to support you more than your family and friends. But, you do need to ask them for help to get it done. Of course, if your ego gets in the way, it will hold you back from asking for help. Get over it. Don't let your shyness, low self-esteem, or anything else stop you from gaining the success you're entitled to. This technique is probably the best grassroots means of marketing and should be practiced regularly throughout the life of your practice.

Before you can ask your family and friends to help you, they have to know exactly what you do so they can accurately describe it to others. It's important to first educate those who you consider your personal advocates - those who know you, like you, trust you, love you, and want the best for you - about the healing work you do. Tell them all about the methods, techniques and modalities you've learned and are using and tell them something about the results you've already achieved.

If they don't know exactly what you're doing in your practice, offer to give them a free treatment. There's nothing better than an actual experience of healing that results in real relief to convince someone of your abilities.

If you can get your family and friends to each refer 1-5 new clients to you each time you send out a mailing to them, you may expect to retain at 1 client for every letter you send within a month or two of asking for help. Depending on how many letters you write, you will be able to establish a nice practice in short order - just through referrals.

However, don't get too excited and go out and buy a new car or a house yet. Life being what it is, you may find that not everyone you send letters to will result in a referral. You may only get a 20-30% response (on the high side) which means that if you send out 20 letters, you may get 4-6 people who will send you one new referral each. However, not everyone who is told about you will respond to the word of mouth and actually make an appointment. So be careful not to count on any one marketing technique alone.

Nonetheless, referrals from friends and family are a good way to start and worth taking the time to follow through on before you even open your doors. It is also a good way to supplement your existing practice if you need more clients to fill your schedule.

You may also find that some people will tell more than one person about the great practitioner you are and the great work you do. Those are ultimately the people you are going to want to cultivate and make sure they keep talking about you in glowing terms throughout your practice. Thank you notes and small, but thoughtful, gifts go a long way towards insuring their continued goodwill towards you.

Also remember that while you might want to start off your practice with a large mailing to all of your friends and family members, you don't have to do it all at once. Consider sending out a small number of letters a week. It spreads the work out over time and takes the burden off you. Make sure you still send out all of the letters you intended to send out at the outset. You'll find that as you get in the habit of making your mailings regularly, it gets easier to do and it becomes a productive habit that you'll look forward to because you know it will result in new clients for you and your practice.

2.   Introductory Letter

The introductory letter to family and friends is how you actually go about asking them for their help. As mentioned before, it's a good idea to remind them of the techniques and modalities you use and tell them about the results you've achieved for others so far. Perhaps the inclusion of a testimonial about the improvement in one or more of your clients' health would be helpful and motivational for others to read. They'll also feel more secure in recommending your services to others if they know how prior clients have benefitted with your help.

Here is a sample letter of what you may wish to consider using if you are about to open your practice and want to "prime the pump" by asking friends and relatives for initial referrals:

Dear Janice,

I just wanted to send you a note to tell you how things have changed in my life lately. As you may already know, I've decided to open up my very own healing practice in Hicksville, New York. Maria and I worked real hard to put together our center, the Center for Inner Healing. We're going to be opening on October 15th, 2008.

We're planning to build our practice so that we can both work at it full time. As you know, we're both Certified Hypnotists with the National Guild of Hypnotists and Reiki Masters. Maria has become a Master Instructor of Integrated Energy Technique.

We both also use Emotional Freedom Technique or EFT. EFT is a very powerful way to relieve stress for many people (we've helped a number of people overcome panic attacks and phobias recently) and it can help youngsters take tests without worries or fears getting in the way. It works on lots of issues where other techniques often don't help.

We're asking for your help in getting people to come to us because you've known us for so long and know us better than anyone else. We believe you can trust us. If you know anyone you think could use our help by reducing or eliminating the stress in their life or who wants other relief, we'd very much appreciate it if you'd pass along our names to them. *We've already had excellent success in helping others and we know you'd be proud of what we're doing. Plus, it would help those you know who are in need.*

If you would like to stop by for a free mini-session so you can experience what we're doing first hand, give either of us a call and we'll set something up immediately. We're happy to share what we've learned with you.

Sincerely,

Ted Robinson

P.S. We're having a "Healing Night" for our friends and family on June 22, 2008 and you're invited to attend FREE. We hope you can make it. We'll be sharing our mini-sessions with everyone who attends. Don't miss it. It's a fun night and you'll definitely get something out of it yourself.

Here's another example:

Dear Tom,

This is just a short note to tell you how excited Maria and I are about opening our new healing center in Hicksville, New York. As you know, we've been taking lots of courses over the last few years on healing work and we've become certified Hypnotists with the National Guild of Hypnotists. We also have become Interfaith Ministers as well as Reiki Masters. We do quite a lot of different things to help others heal themselves. Actually, that's our motto: "Helping Others Help Themselves."

We're very excited about the new direction our lives has taken since we've both always wanted to help others and now we're getting the chance to do so.

We ask you to refer anyone you know who needs alternative health care to us. You'll be pleased to know that many who have already seen us have given us glowing testimonials. We've enclosed a few together with this letter just to give you an idea of our results.

We'd also like to invite you to come to a family and friends evening to demonstrate what we do and give everyone a free mini-session so they know exactly how it feels to be worked on by either or both of us. We want you to know what we do so that when you refer someone to us, you can do it with confidence knowing first hand what they're going to experience.

We're having a Family and Friends night on September 1ˢᵗ at 7 PM at our Center and we invite you to join us for free. Give us a call to confirm so we have enough chairs set up to accommodate everyone. It should be a great night together as friends and family.

We look forward to seeing you and demonstrating our expertise to you.

Warmly,
Ted and Maria

3.   Family and Friends Introductory Night

If you're going to ask your friends and family to refer people to you, they should at least be familiar with what you do for people. The best way to have them be fully familiar is to offer free sessions or treatments to them using the very techniques you intend to use on future clients. Personal experience goes a long way when it comes to referring others. Nothing is better than a first-hand testimonial of how much better <u>they</u> felt after being treated by you. If you don't feel you have the time to do full individual treatments, consider offering an introductory open house in which you invite family and friends to your office to demonstrate your healing work and do mini-sessions on them. It's amazing how people will react to seeing healing going on in their presence and there's nothing better than having an actual healing experience to propel them to refer others to you.

4.   Update Letters

If your practice is already underway and you want to infuse it with new clients, consider using an "update letter" to let your friends and family know what you've been doing and tell them about some of the great results you've been getting for people. Nothing breeds success like success and the more successful you are, the more your friends and family will want to send clients to you.

Your friends and family will often have health related conversations with people they know and alternative health care will come up if they're tuned into that type of care. You might want to remind them to mention you and pass on your phone number, email address or website to those who need help or are interested and the rest will take care of itself.

Here's what a sample letter might sound like:

Dear Kathy,

We're pleased to tell you that your efforts have helped us open our practice. We are now in business and we have seen a number of clients. They are telling us things like they have "never felt better" and are "so pleased that we opened the Center." We wanted to take a minute to thank you for sending along referrals to us. We trust they've also told you about their experiences at our Center.

We're proud of all we've done in such a short time and we look forward to doing much, much more for the community. We feel we're offering a very important service to others which has been reinforced by the wonderful responses we've received from our clients.

Nonetheless, we're looking to expand and offer our services to more people. If you know anyone who might benefit from our care, please refer them to us. Not only will we appreciate it, but they will too. You'll also be helping the world because as each person heals themselves and their life, they heal the world at the same time. That's why our motto is "Heal Yourself, Heal the World."

Don't forget, if you ever want us to assist you, we'll be more than pleased to do so at a reduced rate (or for free) since we're friends (family).

Sincerely,
Ted and Maria

You can also use this same method of letter writing to your past and/or present clients. Again, be very careful not to look needy or you will likely lose your professional status quickly. Consider presenting your clients with an opportunity to share what or how they have benefitted through your services. Be careful about this because many people are not willing to share with anyone the fact that they have had something that needed to be treated by any type of professional. It will likely work well with massage or acupuncture practices or similar types of practices in which people benefit without being "sickly" or maladjusted. You might consider pointing out to them that if they remember how badly they felt when they first came to you and how well they felt afterward, they just may want to share that type of benefit with others.

5.   Multiple Letters

Remember to send more than the first letter to your family and friends. Send at least two over a six month period. More if needed during the first year. You'll be surprised and impressed at how many people they will send to you after each of the letters you send them. You might also want to consider following up with a quick phone call to thank them for their referrals. Of course, whenever you call them, ask if your letter is an imposition or irritating in any way and make a note if they say it is. Never overdo anything when it comes to this, but always remember most of them want to help you and by asking for their help, they know exactly what they can do to help you. Personal referrals will often last as much as a year or more. It feels great when you receive that phone call from a new client and they tell you it was a friend or family member who referred them to you. Always call or write a thank you card to the person that referred a new client as soon as you get their referral. By the way, always have a supply of Thank You cards in your office so that you can immediately write them out instead of putting it off until you buy the cards. Otherwise, you'll invariably get too busy and they'll never get sent out.

Here is a sample letter:

Dear Rita,

I just wanted to catch you up on what we've been doing lately at our Center. We thought you would be interested because of the people you've sent to us. We are now offering weekly group sessions. I'm doing Emotional Freedom Technique each Wednesday evening and Maria is doing Meditations every Tuesday at noon. She's recently started to do another group on Hypnosis and another on the Course in Miracles, so you can see how things are expanding. We're very excited about all this growth in our practice. We're both seeing people individually as well and we want to increase the attendance at our groups and increase our client base for individual sessions so we can help even more people.

If there is anyone you come across who you think could benefit from what we do, please be sure to refer them to us. We know we will be able to help them as we've helped so many others. We've gotten a number of positive testimonials, a few of which we've enclosed for you to look at.

Thanks for all your trust in us.

Warmly,
Ted

6.   A Handwritten Note on Each Letter

It's <u>important</u> to include a handwritten note to anyone you are sending a typed or form letter to at the top and/or bottom of the page. It will make the note even more personal than the letter itself and keep you in closer touch with the person you're writing to. Even if it is only a few words to that special someone, it makes a difference because you've reconnected with them energetically and they can feel it and see it in your handwritten words. You may mention something specific or make an offer for them to come in for a complimentary session or ask them to attend a group that you're teaching so they can get a better understanding and appreciation for what you're doing in your practice. Whatever it is you offer, make sure you do it from the heart and make it sincere.

Here are some examples of handwritten notes you can use:

Hi Drew,
Hope all is well with you. Let's get together soon to catch up.
All my best,
Ted

Hi Joe,
Although we haven't spoken in awhile, you're in my thoughts more than I can tell you. Give me a call when you're available so we can get together. Or come to one of my groups for free to see what we're doing these days. This stuff really works well!

Hope to see you soon.
Ted

Hey Joe,
Thanks for thinking of me.
See you soon,
Ted

Hi Karen,
Thanks for your continued trust in my services and abilities. I appreciate it.
Thanks,
Ted

Hi Mary,
Thanks for your continued trust in me.
Thanks,
Ted

As I've said before, it's always a good idea to follow up with a telephone call even if they don't call you. That way they'll know you are actually interested in them and want to see them. You should also follow up with an actual visit. Make the time (and usually you have more time at the beginning of your practice) so you can cement everything you said in your card or letter. Make sure to focus your talk about them as much as you can before telling them anything about the referrals they sent. Then, when they ask what you've been up to lately, tell them what you're doing. Make sure to thank them for their referrals again. Ask them if you can refer people to their business and what type of people you can send them.

Here's a short synopsis on how to get referrals from family and friends:

• Prepare a friendly and warm letter announcing or updating your family, friends and other people you know about how you are opening a practice or about the status of your practice. Make it an exhaustive mailing list and then later reduce it down as you see who refers people to you and who doesn't. Don't forget that many times someone won't initially refer anyone to you and then later on, they will. Don't be too quick to eliminate them from your list.

• Your letter should be friendly because you're writing to your family and friends. Make sure you tell them a lot about your practice so that they will know what and who they're referring others to in the future. They want to help you. Give them the information they need to do so. Be careful that you don't sound like you're trying to sell them something.

• A handwritten note at the top or bottom of the page will make your letter more personal. Include their nicknames and yours.

• Follow-up with a phone call a week to ten days later. Invite them to your office or center for a treatment or an open house night for friends and family members to show them what you do firsthand. You can explain everything you're doing and tell them how they can take advantage of it and/or refer their friends.

• You can explain to them the type of client you think would benefit most from your treatments. You can also ask if they can think of anyone that could use your help.

You'll be surprised at how many people will refer new clients to you with this system. It takes a lot of work, but it is well worth it to start your practice off and to keep the pump primed.

You may choose to adopt any part of the sample letters. Change it or make up your own letter any way you think will sound most like you and your speaking voice. Make sure that whatever it is you settle on sounds like you and <u>only</u> you. Your friends and relatives know you better than you know yourself at times, so keep your letter light and easy going. Don't make it sound like you're needy or hurting. In fact, <u>there should be no whining or begging at all</u>. Don't try to "guilt" anyone into anything. Use only a short, friendly letter asking them to refer people to you that they think would be helped by what you do. Then watch the results.

7. Testing Your Letter - What Does <u>That</u> Mean?

It's important to test everything you do in marketing. Testing means that unless your first letter gets exceptional responses, it is likely that you can make it better. In order to know what will make it better, you need to test various alternatives. Change the contents of your letter or some other part of the process and monitor your results again. This is called **testing** and it takes time to see the results. Remember, change **only one thing at a time**. That way, you can tell what change worked for you. If you change two or more things in your letter or in how you followed-up with a phone call, then you will never know exactly which part was effective. Once you get a good result, stick with that version until it no longer works. Don't mess with success.

Remember to keep your letters current with what you're offering and change it when you see the response taper down.

8.   Thank You Card Follow-up

It is always a great touch to send a thank you card to everyone who has sent you a referral - <u>for each referral</u> - <u>at the time</u> each referral comes in. It not only thanks them, which is a gracious and appropriate thing to do, it also reinforces their commitment to making more referrals to you. It also speaks volumes about you for taking the time to thank them. It will give them a chance to follow-up themselves with their friend and see how they felt about you. Assuming they feel good, their conversation with their friend will further reinforce their commitment to refer clients to you and it gives them an opportunity to bask in the glow of having done a good deed for their friend. And don't forget to also write thank you notes to clients who refer clients to you. All the same reinforcements apply to each of them.

Make sure to keep a supply of attractive thank you cards on hand so they can go out as soon as a referral comes in to you. That way, you won't forget to do it and they get immediate reinforcement for their kindness towards you. I suggest that you buy a couple of different types of Thank You cards so that if you wind up sending more than one to the same person, each one is unique to them, instead of the same old stock card that everyone gets every time. In fact, you could easily mark each type of card's box with 1st, 2nd, 3rd, etc. so you make sure you don't send the same card twice to the same person. That little personalization always helps them feel special and everyone likes to feel special.   There are also computerized card companies like sendcardsout.com that will send your thank you notes out in your own handwriting and you can make them up on your own computer and send them out remotely by using the Internet (this is covered in another area of the book), but those type of set-ups are somewhat costly and often require a monthly minimum of cards to be sent. It does work well though and their product line is quite nice. However, the least expensive alternative is to buy different Thank You notes and keep them in your office and send them out when it is appropriate.

If someone sends you referrals repeatedly, then it's time to do something special in return. A gift card or a small bouquet of flowers initially or something else that is thoughtful and unique will do the trick. If they continue to send you referrals, then a complimentary dinner or tickets to a Broadway show would be a great way to show your appreciation. You'll find that this type of largess will be repaid many times over. The more you extend yourself, the more others will extend themselves toward you. One thing to remember, however, is to not be attached to whether or not they continue to refer new clients to you. If they only send you one person, always remark to them about how grateful you are to them. Never remind them to send more people, unless it is in another letter to them.

9. Write an Introductory Letter to Professionals for Referrals

This letter is similar in nature to the one we discussed about family and friends, however, it's sent to professionals in other fields and it is not quite so personal sounding. By writing to professionals, you give them the opportunity to learn more about you, what you do and why they should consider referring clients to you.

Before you can contact other professionals, you first have to get their names, addresses and what they do in their practices. To put together a list, you can either look through your local telephone directory or by searching the Internet. To look them up on the Internet, go to a search engine like Google or Yahoo and search for the type of professional you want to write to. You might search for therapists, psychologists, psychiatrists, Certified Social Workers, Social Agencies, counselors, life coaches, etc. Once you've done that, you can add additional words to your search which makes it more specific, like the city or state you practice in or any area you want to contact. That way, you can limit any search by locale as well as the type of work they do.

The results will give you a number of names and postal or email addresses. While this might be considered to be Spam on the Internet, there is a specific now in effect called the CANSPAM Law of 2003. Basically, it holds that you must follow various parameters if you intend to send unsolicited emails out to others and solicit anything from them. Of course, there are exemptions for religious and political messages, but any other solicitation must have a working opt-out mechanism that allows recipients to simply click on it and it will take them off your email list. Secondly, you must have an accurate and true name on your email so the recipient knows who it is from. Third, to be safe, you should follow the 80/20 rule which basically holds that in any email you send, 80% of it should consist of information and content and only 20% should be a solicitation of any nature. That way, you can always prove that your basic purpose was to educate and inform, rather than to simply seek employment for your services or to sell something.

You may also send to previous clients new content and even solicitations as long as you give them a viable means of opting-out easily.

While there are other criteria, these are the highlights of the Act and are the most important ones to follow. If you think you may be in any danger of violating the Act, such as by sending out hundreds of thousands of emails to lists that you've bought and have no idea of who they are or where they're from, then you should check the CANSPAM Act of 2003 on Wikipedia.com for more complete and accurate information.

Your letter should sound something like this:

Name of professional
Address

Re: Introductory Educational Meeting of Professionals

Dear Dr. Simon:

I'm pleased to inform you that we have opened our office, the Center for Inner Healing, in Hicksville, New York. Our practice addresses the "inner healing" of our clients on their quest towards peace of mind and calmness. We have developed a number of modalities to assist others in eliminating the issues that hold them back and cause them emotional pain. We primarily use Emotional Freedom Technique, but we also use

Hypnosis, Integrated Energy Therapy (IET) and Reiki along with a few other things. Primarily, we work on the spiritual/emotional aspects of each person, their "inner self," to ultimately address the outer self and relieve stress.

I'm pleased to inform you that we are holding an evening for Professionals to introduce them to Emotional Freedom Technique, one of the newest techniques developed to eliminate negative emotions and self-limiting beliefs. We've had ten years of experience in working with people with EFT and have seen some extraordinary results made in a very short period of time. We are introducing this wonderful technique to Professionals so they can see the benefits of it and perhaps adopt it in their own practices. We are also doing this to expose you to our expertise in these areas so that whenever you become interested enough to learn it, you will consider attending our teaching program. Of course, if you have anyone who doesn't respond to normal talk therapy or other modalities and they've run into a wall of internal resistance, you may wish to refer them to us as a last resort. We've been very successful in those type of situations and we always protect our referring professionals' reputations.

Reservations are now being taken for September 2, 2008 at 7 PM. The Introductory Evening will last only until 8:30 PM so it won't take a big bite out of your personal time. Give us a call now and reserve your FREE seat since space is very limited. You'll get personalized attention and information. Many professionals have evening hours and if you are interested in learning about what we do but this date and time conflict with your hours, please let us know and we'll do our best to schedule another meeting at a time convenient for you. Call us and speak to our appointment secretary or one of us directly. We'll be glad to answer any questions you may have.

We look forward to hearing from you and seeing you at the meeting.

Respectfully yours,

THEODORE W. ROBINSON

By writing to professionals in your area, you are letting them know what you do for people and that you are available in the same area. Most of them will put it away in the back of their minds and if the need ever arises, they'll send someone along to you. It may take awhile, but it will happen if they can't do any more for their client and they are at their wit's end.

Second, by writing the letter to professionals, you automatically establish yourself as a peer and a professional in their eyes. Think about it. You're writing to them on their level and offering to teach them something they more than likely have heard about and wondered about - for FREE. That's a big benefit that doesn't cost them anything. People usually like that concept and will take advantage of it if they can.

10. Write Holiday and Birthday Cards to Your Clients

Your practice members will not only appreciate it, they will often respond with cards over the years which helps to build and maintain relationships with practice members. This builds rapport, loyalty and continuity with your practice members and that's a good thing all around. In effect, you are building community and that community will hold together and support itself and your office if it feels the connection. Sending out cards of this nature, while sometimes considered a bit cliched, is still worthwhile and it ultimately pays off in the end. You'll be surprised at how many people will mention the nice card they received from you when they speak to you. Again, you can use cards that you've purchased in bulk to keep your costs down, but then it becomes quite labor intensive to keep up with them over time. Or you may wish to use sendoutcards.com and you can do it all online.

The sending of birthday cards can be scheduled on your computer so clients get the cards on time, it makes them feel special and remembered by you. However, make sure you have a relationship with them or they will view it as crass commercialization. There's nothing better than keeping in touch with the members of your practice through regular greeting cards and the money that's spent on the card and postage will be paid back in loyalty and attendance over time.

The website SendOutCards.com, and others like them, can send out a personalized message on a card you've chosen at a reasonable cost per card.

It might be worth the cost considering they are doing all the mailing and envelope stuffing. While SendOutCards.com in particular can be structured as a multilevel marketing deal and some aspects of it can have a minimum monthly expenditure, you can also just do it as a consumer using their service. If you make a commitment to building your practice, using a service like this one might make more sense than burdening yourself or your staff on a regular basis sending out cards for all occasions. They may cost a bit more initially, but the cards are very high quality and they go out with a customized message on each one which you simply type with your order. I've received their company's cards from different people and the cards have never failed to impress me.

Of course, you must fully investigate all aspects of this type of mailing system before entering into it. It can be used as a money making device or simply as a means to send out cards regularly. I recommend this type of function whether you use this particular website or not because when clients, friends or family get an individualized card with a personalized message to them, it is impressive and it keeps your name in their mind after that. Once they have your name stuck in their mind, whenever they need your services, they know who to call - you!

11.   Send out a Quarterly <u>Printed</u> Newsletter

While it is important to send out a newsletter by email fairly often, it is also important to send out a printed newsletter occasionally - at least quarterly. By sending a hard copy newsletter out to your clients, you have the chance to put something in writing into their homes that they will look at for months to come. That's because a printed newsletter, if its done right, will be valued enough by the recipient to keep in their homes for later review. It also gives you enough time to put together a dynamite newsletter rather than a rapidly thrown together email newsletter, so the content should be captivating, entertaining and instructive to your readers.

Make sure to include some case histories about people you've seen so that your readers will know exactly what it is you do. That way, if they see something interesting that applies to them or a member of their family, they'll know who to call. It is best to include only new content so that those who have been regularly reading your e-newsletters will not be turned off to your hard copy and dispose of it without reading the rest of it.

A printed newsletter will also give you the opportunity to expose new products that you've produced so your client base can see them in print rather than on a computer screen. Somehow it makes them appear more substantial than just by being shown on a computer screen.

It's usually best to keep your printed newsletter no more than four pages, printed on both sides. That way, you can have it printed on one sheet of ll" x 17" inch paper and have it folded in half and then folded in half again and sealed for mailing. If you later want to increase the number of pages, you can either add a single sheet of 81/2"x11" paper for the middle two pages or you can add another 11"x17" paper and add four pages of printed material and staple it in the middle.

If you have any reservations about writing your own articles or simply don't feel you have the time to write them yourself, there are a number of websites on the Internet that either sell or offer free articles from other authors that you can use in your newsletter. Here's a sampling of them:

articlebase.com
articlebiz.com
articlecircle.com
amazines.com
articlecity.com

You may also wish to make an arrangement with other website owners to exchange articles with them or have guest authors write an article for you to be posted either on each others' website or in one another's printed newsletters. Of course, no matter who you use, you should always attribute authorship to the person who wrote the article or made the quotation you use.

You may wish to add letters to the editor or questions and answers to your newsletter, depending upon how long you want it to be and how much time you wish to devote to it. A quaint saying, quote or motto is also helpful to give your practice members something interesting to read. Don't forget to include at least one new testimonial each time you send out a newsletter.

You should determine how many newsletters a year you want to distribute. That way, you'll know about how much they will cost to send out and you can budget enough money to accomplish it. Or you may realize that it is going to cost you too much to meet your goal and have to cut back the number you send out. Either way, it is best to have at least three newsletters "in the can" before you issue the first one. That way, when your office traffic starts to improve, you'll still have enough backups to be able to put a new one out while you're busy. There is nothing worse than publishing a newsletter with big goals and a regular posted schedule and then fail to meet your own schedule. It is better to not have any scheduled and tell people you intend upon issuing it "irregularly" so they don't come to expect it. That way, they are not let down and you're not pressured.

Remember, the primary purpose of a newsletter is to keep in touch with your clients and keep your name in their minds even when you don't see very much of them. If you accomplish that alone, you've maintained your connection with them and if they need your services they'll be much more likely to contact you for an appointment.

12.   Send out a Quarterly Calender of Events to All Practice Members

Prepare a printed Quarterly calender of events for your practice so that people can see in advance what you have planned for your office and practice. That way, they can post it on their refrigerator and plan to be there for events that interest them and they'll know when you are expecting to be closed. It also gives you a means of keeping your office in their mind and your name in their face every time they open their refrigerator. Consider a simple one sheet, two sided colored paper that they might want to post in their home so they'll see it regularly. You can also put out reminders on the reverse side of new things you're doing or anything else you're sponsoring in your office during that quarter. It's a simple device, but it works effectively because it gives each practice member something concrete in their hand to view.

You may also wish to enclose your calender of events along with your printed newsletter in order to reduce your costs and give your clients a reason to retain both of them for three months at a time.

FOLLOW-UPS AND FREEBIES

13.   Make Follow-up Phone Calls to Clients after Treatments

This is perhaps the best method for naturally showing people you care about them and their welfare. A simple call on the same evening of or the next morning after seeing someone goes a very long way in client relations. While it takes a time commitment, it will yield great results. Clients truly appreciate it and it doesn't take a lot of time. It builds rapport with your practice members and cements in their minds that you are concerned about them. It effectively makes them part of your practice by showing them more than the normal professional concern.

Make your call short, just to check on how they're feeling and if they feel better. Once you get a yes, you can move on to the next call. If a question arises, answer it succinctly and move on again. Don't let them bog you down, yet show your concern. If they do have a problem, then handle it on the spot or ask them to come see you as soon as possible. It's a very helpful mechanism to build your practice and it will lead to far greater satisfaction levels in your practice members and their families. It will also lead to referrals to third parties.

14.   Offer a Free Mini-session

While this may not apply to every type of holistic practice, if you want to jump start your practice, you may find that it is worthwhile to offer free mini-sessions to anyone new who shows an interest. To do this, you first must advertise such an event in one of the many ways outlined in this book. Consider flyers, mailings, email or any of the other suggestions. Make sure to have them reserve a spot in advance so you don't get inundated all at once and have to turn people away. If you make up a schedule and keep to it, everyone will get the opportunity to be treated and have a short experience of what you do during a normal session. Once they've experiences some sort of relief due to your help, they'll make an appointment as soon as they feel they need more help with their condition.

You may also find specific people who are sending you a large number of referrals after you've been open for awhile. In such a case, you might offer a free mini-session or full personal session for them, a family member or a person of their choice. If you do this, it is important to subtly let them know how valuable such a session is based upon what you charge others for a full session. Don't be afraid to build it up to its fullest - as long as you don't exaggerate beyond its true value. These type of sessions should convey your heartfelt appreciation and gratitude and don't ever skimp on your treatment just because it's free. Give them the entire treatment and they'll be talking about it for months to others. It's well worth doing it right.

15. Conduct an Open House with Free or Reduced Rate Treatments

Holding an introductory open house is a great way to expand your office and expose your abilities to the public. If you do it right, it can make a big difference to your practice and speed up the process of extending your reputation in your area. It can also be used as a Grand Opening if you're just opening your practice. The first rule is: <u>Don't skimp on what you offer at an open house</u>. Impress everyone who shows up with your graciousness and expansiveness - without looking too garish or over-the-top.

When preparing for an Open House or a Grand Opening, make sure that you give yourself plenty of time so that everything in your place is cleaned up and looking brand new before you hold it. There's nothing worse than a half-baked event where you're still cleaning up or working on something. It looks unprofessional and incomplete and that's not the image you want people getting the first time they visit your office. Remember, there's never a second opportunity to make a first impression. The first impression is the one that stays with your visitors. It sets the tone for everything that follows.

Next, when preparing for an event, make sure that you put out a press release well in advance so that the local papers will carry it for you <u>for free</u> and in a timely fashion. You may also wish to take out some print and radio advertising about your Open House so that even more people will know about it. Newspapers are usually more prone to printing something about your office if you also place some advertising with the paper.

Make sure to send out invitations to everyone - people you know, may know you, may have heard of you, or even those who have never heard of you. Send to those business people you've been meeting at breakfast meetings. Send to as many local residents as possible. Send to anyone and everyone you can think of so that by the time the appointed day arrives, you'll have more people than you can fit. Make it an exciting event so that the energy of your Open House will carry on for weeks to come. Get people talking about the event itself and it will keep them talking about you. Remember, word of mouth is still the king of advertising. Give people something good to talk about and you'll be the talk of the town for a long time. Then, all you have to do is back it up with professional workmanship and abilities and your practice will flourish.

16. Teach Your Specialty at Alternative Health Care Organization Conferences

Many holistic and alternative groups have annual conventions for their members to attend so they can stay current with the latest technique or just stay in touch with others in their area of interest. Many of these conventions have turned into an educational opportunity to gain continuing education credits which means they must have qualified teachers to share their knowledge with attendees. If you want to become well known in your area of interest, it makes sense to become a teacher at the convention of your choice at which you can showcase your knowledge and expertise.

First, decide which conventions you wish to teach at and then its normally best to attend at least one of them beforehand to make sure it's the type of group with which you wish to be associated. If you don't know how to find conventions of this nature, type in "alternative conferences", "CAM conferences" or "Alternative Health Care Conferences". You may also wish to review centralized listings of such conventions or conferences at "allconferences.com" or "hypnosisresearchinstitute.org" to find additional conference and convention listings.

Once you've decided upon which conferences and conventions you want to lecture at, make sure you make up your annual schedule ahead of time so you don't have any conflicts between them. Call or write their convention headquarters and ask for an application. Many already post their applications on their websites for ease of access and to attract new speakers all the time.

Submit your proposals to the conferences or conventions you want to lecture at that have an interest in what you do. Write up a proposal that is consistent with what they're already looking for and you'll find you're in more demand than you ever imagined.

If you're a hypnotist, offer to teach a workshop at one of the Hypnosis Conventions that have grown up around the country. If you do energy work or any related modality, try the Energy Psychology Convention or any other type of convention that serves your purpose. They are all looking for people to speak who have authored a book or who do a unique technique to showcase at their convention.

The speakers are the ones that draw the crowds to the event and the organizers know that. They want the best speakers to draw the biggest crowds because that makes the most money and increases their power within the alternative community. Become the obvious expert in your particular field and get yourself as much exposure as you can and they'll want you to lecture at their function.

Look at what the conference organizers have accepted in the past. Look at their overall theme for the following year and then draft up two or three different proposals taking different tacks on what you have to offer. Be sure to take some extra time to make them sound professional and interesting to their participants. Remember, organizers are trying to sell their convention as well and an interesting offering list is what brings people to them. It also brings them to see you at the convention, so take whatever time it takes to make a strong presentation.

In this regard, when you do speak at any of these conventions, it is worthwhile to invest additional time to give the listeners more than they expect. You can do this by either doing a Power Point presentation that is filled with colors and different types of moving images or you may wish to distribute some pamphlet, papers or cards that carry some pertinent information about your speech and has your name and contact information on it. That way, when they return home from the convention, they will have something on hand to review and it will have your name and contact information on it. You'll be surprised at how many people will contact you months and years later about the simple hand-out you left in their hands. It also leaves them with a good feeling that they received more than they ever expected when they attended your lecture.

17. Speak at Local Libraries or Business Groups

Offer to speak about what you do at your local library or business group whenever you can. This will help you reach people who have never heard of you before. Once they've heard you speak, not only will they know who you are, they will know what you do and see you as the obvious expert in that field. Make your initial proposal to the Chief or Head Librarian in person if possible or if you can't, in writing and attach a copy of a professional looking proposed flyer that will interest them and the potential people who you are trying to attract. By doing this, you give the Librarian something to evaluate to see if they think it will appeal to their library's patrons. If they think you will, they'll contact you to schedule your talk and set up ways in which to help you make it more successful. However, don't expect them to actually do much to assist you. You should expect to do all the promotion for your talk on your own and then, if they give you any assistance, it's gravy.

Start out by setting the topic, time, date and cost, if any (most libraries want their talks to be free, but some may allow a small admission fee to defray expenses if you explain that to them in advance). Then, set-up the precise wording of the title of your talk to attract the most people and get it approved beforehand by the library.

Once that's all done, ask if the library has any prohibition about promotion. You don't want to start promoting your talk, only to find that you're stepping on their toes in some fashion later. If they have no specific prohibitions, then use the other ideas in this book to set up your advertising and notices in newspapers, radio, Internet, etc.

Also, it's important to determine if they have any reservations about you offering additional products "in the back of the room" after your talk. If they won't allow any sales, then you may wish to reconsider whether you want to do the talk, since that's an important factor for you. Many experienced speakers won't even do a talk unless they're allowed to distribute their own printed matter and sell "back of the room" items after the talk. Even if the library doesn't allow you to sell anything, it may still benefit you to do the talk because anyone who shows up will learn something from you and you'll be viewed as the obvious expert by a new group of people who then know who to turn to in their times of need.

At the very least, make sure you have a way to collect their email addresses so you can add them to your list. One way to do this is to offer a "door prize" of your book or a free CD or DVD. In order for you to choose a winner for the prize, they must give you an index card (which you will provide to them as they enter the room as part of your packet of information) with their name, address and email on it. After you've done your drawing and given out the book, CD, etc., you are left with names to add to your email list and that's how you will continue to keep in touch with them. By keeping in touch with them, you'll keep your name in their minds and whenever they finally need your services (or one of their friends need them), that's when they'll think of you and call you.

18.   Network with Local Businesses at Their Regular Meetings

Just about every community has a Chamber of Commerce or business association so that they can get together and make business contacts with one another. They often hold breakfast meetings before the start of the day to build rapport and support one another's businesses. Of course, while this takes some time and attention (as well as getting up early), it is often worth it because this is usually the first place other business owners will learn about you in the community and get to know what you do in your practice. If other businesspeople know about you and what you do, they may pass information about you and your practice to their customers. Again, word of mouth is still the most powerful means of advertising. If you get them interested in who you are and what you do, they'll can help spread the word to help your practice grow.

You may even wish to offer a discount to any business owner for the first visit or first month of care with you so they experience whatever it is you do. That way, they have an additional incentive to visit you and recognize your expertise. Once they're satisfied that you are good at what you do, they'll feel that much more comfortable referring others to you.

Whatever you do, if someone shows interest, book an appointment with them immediately. On the spot. Don't hesitate. That way, they've made a commitment to take action and that's what brings in new clients.

If you want to get real adventurous, you can offer a free introductory session to the first three-five members who sign up with you and that will break the ice even quicker. At the same time, it will also quickly build goodwill for your practice.

# 19.	Join Speakers Groups

If you have any fear of public speaking, joining a group like Toastmasters USA is a great way to overcome that fear (of course, using EFT will do it quicker, but this will also work, just a little slower). When you join Toastmasters USA, they have a specific protocol for new members so that each new member gets to speak for short periods of time and are graded by the established members on how well they did. That way, they can improve their speaking abilities and get their message out at the same time. It's a great organization and the protocol works well. Remember, you are also getting an opportunity to expose what you do to a group of people who may never have heard of you or what you do. You will be surprised at how responsive they can be to a strong message with good content.

You can also go to other Toastmasters' Chapters than the one you joined and speak to them as well. That gives you a more varied and diverse audience. The same holds true for Rotary, Lions and most other civic minded groups.

If you're going to speak at any of these type of meetings, it is always a good idea to carry with you extra brochures, business cards and copies of your book, even if you can't display or distribute them in the "back of the room". That way, if anyone shows real interest in you and your talents, you can give them a card, take their email address or even sell them a book after you leave if they are that intent upon learning more. Always be prepared anywhere you go so that you can fulfill others' needs at the very time they ask for more information. Strike while the iron is hot and make a sale or distribute your information. Also, remember to ask for names, addresses and email addresses wherever you speak. It makes the experience more worthwhile to you, but even if you can't get any email addresses, do the talks anyway. You'll enjoy them and it gives you greater exposure.

20. Conduct Charitable Holiday Events

Each year, especially as the Thanksgiving/Christmas/winter season rolls around, many people start to think about helping the needy. This is a perfect opportunity for you get into the giving spirit and get some benefits out of it for your practice.

Hold a food drive for the needy through your office and offer free evaluations or mini-sessions to anyone who brings in a can of food or some other type of food for a food drive. You can also ask for used clothing for a clothing drive or a new gift for a gift drive for needy children.

This does two things at the same time. One, it supplies gifts, food and clothing for the needy which is a good thing no matter what you receive in return. Second, it supplies you with an opportunity to evaluate and/or treat everyone who comes in to see you with a donation, which allows you to determine if they require further assistance from you and your office. If they don't, then all you've spent is a little time evaluating them and building rapport with them so that in the future, if they do need your services, they'll be more prone to using you.

On the other hand, if they do need your services, they've already built an initial level of trust with you because you have joined with them in a common purpose of charity. They're usually happy to use whatever services you offer because they trust you and your expertise even if they have little experience with it. They like what you're doing, have joined with you in a charitable enterprise and hence, already trust you. The rest falls into place quite easily and quickly once you have people's trust and respect.

This is also a great opportunity to obtain free advertisements by sending the local newspapers a press release ahead of time to advise them of your food, toy or clothing drive. That way, you'll reach the entire local population for free because the paper will be alerting them to your charitable event. You can also post flyers all over town, in the supermarket, Laundromat and anywhere else you can think of so that everyone knows what you're doing. Even if you don't get any new clients out of it (which is doubtful), everyone in your local town will know you've done something special and good-hearted and will be that much more interested in supporting you and your practice.

This type of a charitable event is also a way of getting radio, television and cable television announcements for free which will highlight your name and the name of your practice. There is also usually an events calender on every cable channel which will post your charitable event if you send it to them well enough in advance. One more thing is to send notice to the news department of your local broadcast television and/or radio stations a couple of weeks ahead of time so they can schedule an interview with you to improve the public's response to your event. All of these things work together to bring about a successful event and while doing that, you get your name and your practice's name out over the airways or by cable to almost everyone in your area.

While all this may sound somewhat jaded or like the commercialization of a charitable event, this is just an explanation of how to best utilize efforts that you intend upon doing anyway. The fact that others will notice that you and your practice did this for others just inures to your benefit regardless of how much you advertise it.

21.   Teach a Class at the Local Adult Education

Teaching a class at a local adult education will expose your talents and expertise to the local adult population. Yes, it takes some consistent effort to put together a class program and follow through with it but, you'll find it exhilarating to teach a class of new people who are interested and watch them as they grow over the duration of the class.

Not only that, but you'll find that as your class matures into whatever it is you're teaching them, they will hold you in higher esteem each week as they try out whatever they've learned the previous week. As the process continues, you'll notice referrals coming to you from them and their families as they send those they can't help to you - since you are the obvious expert in their eyes. This is important because have sown the seeds of practice development that will give you results for years to come. Plus, it is another great addition to your teaching credentials and curriculum vitae.

22.   Teach a Class at a Local College

Similar to teaching an adult educational class at a local high school, moving up to a community college night school gives you a higher credential than adult education at the high school level. However, having done a class at the local adult education system may very well help you get the job at the college. Recommendations from those who have taken your original class may well turn into what you need to get to teach the class at a community college.

Many community colleges have recently expanded their class offerings to include alternative health care classes and related relaxation classes or healing classes. They usually try to make some sort of distinction between these classes and their traditional scholastic classes, but they're out there offering them nonetheless. All of them need speakers who can offer something to the public that is informative, pertinent to an alternative health care issue and presented in a professional fashion. You could be chosen to be one of those that teach at your local college by simply making an application and displaying your experience and knowledge. You then can spread the word about whatever it is you're doing in your field to an entirely new audience.

There are many obvious benefits to teaching at the college level. While many of these schools may not be on the same level as accredited college courses, they are still being taught at some of those same colleges, so its great for your teaching credentials. It also helps to support your theme of becoming the obvious expert in whatever field of endeavor you've chosen since anyone reviewing your background will simply see you taught at a college level.

More than that, it helps others accept you when you ask for speaking engagements at corporations or elsewhere. When they see your credentials, which include teaching a class at a college in the area, it helps them make a positive determination about you and whatever it is you wish to speak about in their forum.

All of this contributes to you becoming the obvious and accepted expert in the area of your practice. It is an accumulation of accolades that forms a reputation over time.

23.   Volunteer Your Time and Talents to Help Indigent People

Healing those in desperate need who have no other means of being healed is admirable and should be done regularly by you within your community - just to do it. When you volunteer your time and abilities to help indigent people help themselves, you are not only giving back to the community, you are honing your abilities and offering much needed help to those who are most in need. The simple act of doing such volunteer work is reward in and of itself. However, when you do this type of work, the word usually gets around that you not only have the expertise to help others, but you are willing to do so on a voluntary basis. This will inure to your benefit and build your personal reputation within the community.

When you help the indigent from time to time, it goes a long way towards improving community relations. It also says a great deal about you. It builds your reputation within the community and among religious leaders in no time at all. And it is the right thing to do. On top of that, it will often lead to referrals of new clients who can pay you which can help to build your practice and your reputation.

24.   Hold a Free Screening Day for the Public at Your Office

A free screening day is a great way to expose your expertise to the public and sign people up for future work with you. When you are first starting out, this is one of the best methods for practice building because you actually get to speak directly to people that you've never met before and build a rapport with them. This is almost imperative in the holistic field since most holistic practitioners are "hands-on" types and know that by making that connection, they will eliminate the resistance that most people have to healing.

The way to do this is to put out flyers, print and Internet ads that tell people that you're willing to evaluate them in person. You can spend whatever period of time you feel it will take you to do a competent job. It doesn't have to mean a session with them for free. That's what you're trying to get them to make an appointment for within a few days. Only the screening is free. That's the hook. If they like you and feel comfortable with you, then they'll be more than willing to book an appointment and show up.

Even if you have an empty appointment book, don't be too pushy to set up an appointment or they'll think you're needy and reject you. The key is to "be available" without being needy. It's a tightrope to walk initially, but once you get the hang of it, you'll find it is not difficult at all. It is best to be open with everyone and to advise them honestly about their condition. Don't make anything look or sound dire if it is not. Remember, you're building a reputation within the community. How you act with each client reflects who you are. You are completely in charge of how your reputation turns out. Do a professional job and do it well and you'll establish a positive reputation quickly.

25.   Sponsor a Little League Team or Other Sports Team

Sponsoring a Little League team is a great way to get your name on a lot of little kids' uniforms and in the minds of their parents and every parent of every team that plays with them each week during the summer. Depending upon the size of your league, that could mean a few hundred or a thousand people get to remember and root for your name. That can be a good start in marketing if you follow-up with other areas of advertising simultaneously. That means "cross-advertising" in newspapers, local magazines, journals, etc. in which those other eyes see your name again. You can also offer a discounted rate "for all parents of Little League players" as a way to thank them for their support of your Little League team.

Cross marketing adds familiarity that works for you. By giving parents a discount, it gives them an added incentive to come to you. Always make certain that any discount is for a limited time only so they'll take action right away. Then watch to see your results. Again, if they don't break down your doors, try another approach by testing new wordings, offers, etc., until you find the right combination. Keep detailed records after every offer so you know which one works best for you.

If you have questions about how to contact the Little League, you'll find them in your local telephone directory or you can check on an Internet search engine. You can also make it simple and ask another team sponsor how they went about signing up to sponsor a team.

26.   Offer a Free Session to Your Local Church/Temple Leaders

Offering free services to local church and temple leaders are great because they have followings in their spiritual communities. As a result, if you convince them of your abilities and expertise, they are perfect referral agents for future clients. The best way for anyone to become a convert is to experience whatever it is you can do to help relieve them from their stress or pain. Once they've experienced it, they're more than willing to suggest your services to others in their congregations because it helps their followers and also makes them look that much better to them as well.

If you really want to supercharge your practice, offer a specific discount to members of any particular congregation for their first session or for their first month of sessions and you'll see a big influx of new clients coming through your door. Once you are well established, you can change or modify any discounts you've offered in the past due to time constraints and while you may lose a few, you'll also gain many others by that time. This is a great means of building a practice quickly and helping worthy people at the same time.

27.   Make Charitable Contributions

Making charitable contributions should never be done in order to advertise yourself or your practice. However, by making charitable contributions or by offering your time and services, you are nonetheless getting positive publicity for yourself. Of course, the most sincere charitable contribution is done anonymously, but if you're going to put your name on it anyway, you might as well get some mileage out of it. My suggestion is that you make your contributions anonymously as that is the best means of doing the right thing in life and life has a way of repaying you in other ways. Overt contributions should not be used to promote you or your practice. However, it is still important to make charitable contributions whenever you can.

By the way, by making charitable contributions, you are laying the groundwork for abundance in your future. The more you feel sufficiently abundant that you are able to give some away, the more things will come to you since you are already open to the Universe's abundance.

28.   Sponsor a Health Fair for the General Public

While it takes a lot of work, sponsoring a health fair can bring about great benefits for you and your practice. It will not only put you in touch with many other practitioners in your field and related fields, it will also put you on the map as a mover and a coordinator of things in the alternative health care field. As I said before, it does take a considerable amount of work to do it right, but if you're going to do it, make sure to do it right. Once you get it done the first time, you learn from your mistakes and you can do it again with much less effort if you decide to do it again.

Running a health fair takes initial scheduling which means you'll have to check to see which are the best weekends to run so that it won't interfere with holidays, vacation times or long weekends. Not only that, but you must schedule your event so it won't be in conflict with large sporting events like Super Bowl Sunday or the World Series, etc. These are important considerations because if you schedule on a busy weekend, people won't show up and your fair could be under attended.

After scheduling comes planning, advertising, coordinating with many other practitioners in various fields, and a healthy amount of energy to accomplish it all. Then, as the time draws near to actually hold your health fair, you'll certainly have your share of last minute problems and people who want to attend who just never got around to making the reservation. Don't forget those that will want to cancel out at the last minute. You'll have to deal with all of them. The best way to do that is to set up a list of rules and regulations ahead of time and publish them on your website. It is probably best to establish a simple website ahead of time so people can see everything on their own and make up their mind without hassling you with their questions. Of course, expect that they'll ask you questions nonetheless and having a website will help you answer those questions by referring them to the appropriate page on the site whenever they ask a question.

Once you've finished the health fair, you will be a magnet for many people who attended and want to come back again in later years. They will be more prone to talking about you and seeing you in a good light, both of which inure to your benefit in the long run. They will also see you as a leader in the health care field and that always helps you and your image.

WORKING WITH OTHER PROFESSIONALS

29. Offer to Do Introductory Mini-sessions in Other Professional's Offices

Many times, other professionals are struggling with certain clients in their practices and are willing to allow someone else to come in and offer their services if it doesn't conflict with what they already offer. Mini-sessions are a way of doing this without imposing on the existing practice while still infusing some new energy into existing clients. Of course, you have to be very careful how you approach anyone with such an offer since they may interpret it as an attempt by you to take part of their practice away from them.

To offset any such reluctance, make certain that you reassure them that your intent is to add new energy into their practice and assist them with their clients and that you will not interfere or hinder with whatever it is they're already doing. Also, make sure that they know you are not seeking to take any of their clients/patients away from them. Let them keep full control of all record keeping and names and addresses of anyone who sees you while in their office. That way, they'll feel more comfortable with the concept until such time as they see that you are in good faith. Once you've built a rapport and they start to see an increase in their own practice's numbers, then you'll be in a better position to work out any kinks between you. If it doesn't work out that way, then you can simply leave and be done with it. Either way, the people you see will have experienced your abilities and expertise and that always carries the day in the long run. If they liked what they experienced, they'll make the effort to find you even if you leave that practice.

30. Volunteer to Be Part of a Discussion Group or Round Table Symposium

By becoming part of a round table discussion or specific symposium with other professionals on a particular topic that you work with or which is related to your field, you will be viewed by both the public and professionals as an expert in your field. In fact, your inclusion in any group discussion can be a very effective way of being viewed as an expert among experts. The primary threshold to initially get past is being invited to participate. Once you've been asked to take part in any discussion group, you're part of the experts who many people come to see and listen to for their opinions.

The key is to be viewed as enough of an expert to be asked in the first place. You need to have a large enough following to be recognized or have sufficient professional credentials to justify people attending to see you and the others who are involved. The best way to accomplish that is to volunteer your speaking services to any group having such a discussion and submit your biography or *curriculum vitae* so they can see who you are from your history. It would also help to refer them to any mention of you on Google.com and/or Yahoo.com or any other search engine that carries your name, and any noteworthy mention of you.

Of course, one of the best ways of gaining their notice is to draft a submission packet containing all your information and submitting it along with a letter volunteering your attendance at any such discussion group. Then follow-up by calling or having someone who is close to the invitation committee call on your behalf and explain why you would be appropriate for the symposium.

One other noteworthy means of gaining recognition is to befriend someone who is already a member and have them recognize you for the work you are doing.

31. Offer Introductory Educational Meetings for Professionals to Obtain Referrals

This is a unique way of introducing yourself and your abilities to other professionals in your area who may not know much about you. If you do this right, it could mean endless referrals from those very professionals who presently think they are in competition with you. By offering to teach them some small part of what you do, it asserts that you are expert enough to have something to teach educated professionals. However, if you can get them into your sphere of influence and get them to recognize that you have something unique to offer that they don't yet have, they will come to you for instruction and hold you in high esteem if you can carry it off.

Of course, it takes a substantial standard of care to be able to carry this off, but if and when you do, you'll have established yourself as an expert on or above their level. If you can also do things that they can't do, they'll be more likely to send their troubled clients to you when they can't handle them effectively. A good example is when another professional cannot handle a specific type of malady and discovers that you can. He/she can discover this information while you teach them whatever it is you do. Once they discover it and develop a comfort level and trust with you, the next time someone comes through their door with that particular condition, you can bet you'll be getting a phone call from that client/patient or the health provider themself. Most therapists or health givers simply want their patients/clients to get better quickly and if they can't do it, they'll usually send them to someone who can help them. That could be you in the future.

To accomplish this, the first thing to do is determine what it is you want to teach to other professionals. Once you've decided upon your topic, then it is time to formulate a list of who you're going to invite. You must realize that most won't necessarily be interested because of their own built-in prejudice against anyone who doesn't hold their level of degrees. That old ego is always watching to make sure that they remain number one in everyone's eyes. However, it has been my experience that after awhile, certain professionals who have integrity actually get tired of doing what they've always been taught when it doesn't help their patients/clients. That's when the ones with integrity will turn to almost anything else to accomplish their ends of getting their patients/clients better. That's when they'll turn to other alternative practitioners seeking the key to helping others. That's when they're willing and interested in meeting you to see what it is that you can do to help.

Don't forget those professionals are also very aware that many, many people have been turning to alternative and holistic health care, even though they have no health insurance benefits to cover the cost of it. They are willing to spend out-of-pocket money for relief from pain and peace of mind and that is unprecedented in the medical model field where insurance coverage is king.

What that means is that the alternative approach is starting to make big inroads into the general public's mind and those professionals are feeling the pinch financially and egotistically. They are first going to want to fight back, but then they're going to want to find out more so that they can eventually provide alternative health care in conjunction with allopathic care, hoping it will make them even more powerful and in demand. But what they often don't know is that alternative health care providers have a different approach which more than likely won't work as well for them. Alternative health care providers have humility and they don't talk down to their clients as a general rule. This is a very basic benefit that helps alternative health care providers maintain their clients and heal them quicker.

32. Speak at Local Chapters of Different Types of Health Care Organizations

Offer your services at a local chapter of various types of health care organizations. This is important because you get the chance to share what you know and build your name among people who are more likely to be interested in you and your topic. Their members are already interested in health care issues or they wouldn't be members in the first place. Most organizations meet monthly and need speakers to fill their schedule. They are more than happy to receive an offer from you to speak to them and fill one of their open slots.

However, if you choose to speak at such a group, make sure that whatever you're speaking about is relevant to what they're interested in so you draw a crowd. Otherwise, you could show up all prepared and nobody shows. That's not fun. Make sure to tailor the title of your talk to their interest and then show them how what you do works with it.

For instance, since I primarily practice Emotional Freedom Technique but want to give speeches to hypnosis groups as well, I developed a new way to do a hypnotic induction using EFT. That way, I had something that expanded what they already knew and that made it a draw for many of the regular members to show up and perhaps learn something new that can help them in their practices. Remember, it is most important whenever you're dealing with the public, or anyone else for that matter, to offer something that appeals to them and what they want to learn. Otherwise, you can have the best speech in the world, but nobody shows up because they don't see what they're going to get out of it. Make your speech about what the listeners want to hear and you'll always be remembered as a great speaker.

On the plus side, speaking to smaller groups can be quite enjoyable since you get to meet new people and they get to learn from you. Such a speaking engagement gives you the opportunity to address them as an expert in your field and then, in the future, if they need information regarding something in that field, they know who to go to or who to send clients to when they can't handle it. If they see you as that expert by the time your talk is completed, you've accomplished the first task you've set out to do.

The second, and perhaps the most important task, is to "harvest" email addresses from everyone that attends. This helps you build your email list which is integral to your practice development. An especially good way to do this is to give something away either as a door prize or a raffle in which anyone who wants to be eligible submits a piece of paper with their name, address, telephone number and email address on it (at the very least, their name and email address). After you've given away a copy of a book or some introductory service, you are left with a group of names and emails you can add to your list all for the very minimal cost of a book to you. It's a great trade-off and well worth the effort. Also, people love a raffle or anything free.

Remember, it's all about them and when they get something for free, they go home happy.

33. Organize a Convention Within Your Specialized Area

By offering to organize a convention of like minded professionals, you will be establishing yourself as a leader in your field. It has been done by a few alternative professionals and they have actually made their reputations based upon their work as convention leaders. As an organizer, you get to establish the rules and regulations and to present awards to deserving people. This will help establish you as one of the leaders in your field by your peers. Beyond that, it brings great attention to you and your field of endeavor and helps to establish your field as a competent area of practice.

Organizing practitioners in your field as a professional organization will also inure to the benefit everyone. This is how all the established organizations started and there's always room for improvement and expansion in this area. While it does take a lot of work, it is well worth it in the long run if you want to become the established leader in your field of endeavor.

There are many National and International Associations that sponsor conventions and the best way to consider how it is done is to attend a few and observe them in action. In fact, the best way to learn how to do it is to volunteer to assist them as they run their convention. Study how they do everything, down to the smallest nuance. Collect and study the catalogs they distribute and follow their lead. Don't try to re-invent the wheel at first. Instead, simply enhance it by taking a different tack and doing it better.

To do it better, the most important thing is to attract the very best speakers and teachers. If you can do that, you'll almost guarantee a following and that's what the speakers invariably want so they can reach more people themselves. Everything has to work together when planning and carrying out a convention. Don't forget, doing the first one is the hardest to carry off. After you've completed the first one, the rest will fall into place with little difficulty and you'll know what not to do the next time. What worked and what didn't. While this is a long shot suggestion, don't completely eliminate it from your prospects since you never know ahead of time where you're going to wind up. A few convention leaders started out practicing a healing profession and eventually wound up running healing conventions and bringing relief to far more people than if they kept to their individual practice. This can also lead to leadership within your field of interest and that can help you bring about greater change in society if you use it effectively.

34.   Offer an Affiliate Program to Others

Affiliate programs are a great way to sell your products and advertise your services. They are a pretty simple concept, but take a bit of work to set up than it may appear on the surface. An affiliate program first requires that you attract enough people who are interested in your work and products who want to share it with others for their own profit. There may be many out there who are interested in doing exactly that because they simply want to make a profit and they'll latch on to anyone or anything to do so. Once they have something posted on their website, it is pure profit for them. It might be better to steer clear of them.

On the other hand, there are those out there who will be so impressed with your work that they will want to share it with others and are more than willing to do so just for the pleasure of doing it. However, to make sure they follow through with it, you can offer them a means to make a profit by using your products through an affiliate program and that will usually make things go easier.

An affiliate program is one in which your affiliates offer your products to the world through their practice and/or websites. To do this, you'll first have to have sufficient products to offer them for sale. That means you'll have to have books, CDs, DVDs, teleseminars, podcasts and other products that they can advertise and sell for you. Once you have enough of an array of products, you can offer them to affiliates at a discount if they advertise them on their websites. However, always make sure that whatever it is they're selling for you will actually be purchased through or fulfilled by your website or fulfillment facility. That way, you can make sure the products go out in the proper fashion and you'll also eventually capture the email of the person buying your product so you can directly contact them again later with a follow-up offering of new products.

It also insures that you are in control of the money and the fulfillment process, insuring that the products go out in a timely fashion as well as being able to keep the accounting straight on all sales. Of course, you'll have to have some sort of accounting computer program available to you to use for your affiliate program, but they are already available on the net and you can again find them through Google by typing in "Affiliate Programming" or similar words.

Remember, affiliate programs are one of the best means of building a network or community of people interested in the same thing and working for the same purpose. It also builds loyalty from your affiliates because they are getting paid by you for offering your products and once they post it to their website, it takes them almost no work at all after that. They are then interested in helping you build your image and reputation, so they can build their product line and income through you. An affiliate program is a win/win proposition all around.

HANDOUTS AND PROMOTIONAL MATERIALS

35.   Prepare a Professional Business Card That Does More

Business cards are your calling card to the world. They should clearly and unequivocally impart who you are, what you do and where to find you in person <u>and</u> on the Internet. You can take different approaches to having your business cards printed based upon the image you wish to present to prospective clients. A conservative approach is to have your card look like a doctor, chiropractor or lawyer and make it very austere with a Times Roman font and a gold embossed image or symbol that fits whatever it is you're practicing. Or you can take a more adventurous approach and have your card designed consistently with your logo or letterhead, using colors and graphics. You may even choose to include a photograph of yourself if you think that will attract more people to you.

You may also wish to include the specifics of what you practice on the front and/or back of the card so that they may see options available to them and perhaps see something that they were always interested in, but never knew where to find it before seeing it on your card.

On the other hand, it is usually best to keep the number of modalities limited on your card so that prospective clients don't see you as a "jack of all trades and a master of none." Instead, have separate cards for separate techniques or modalities which is more likely to make you look like an expert in each field. Most people can't accept the premise that you could be great at more than one thing in this lifetime, even if it is true.

Another approach is to put the client's next appointment date and time on the back of your card. Many professionals do that because it's a practical means of reminding them of their next appointment and keeping their name in their client's mind. That way, clients see your name regularly and they can give your card away to others if they want to refer clients to you.

Don't forget to give away more than one card when giving them to anybody. This will give them extras to give away to their friends when they talk about you later. If they throw it away, it doesn't matter. Take the chance and offer them two or three at a time. It often works.

A business card is a very basic, powerful, marketing tool because you and your personality are directly related to them. And the numbers connected to them are compelling. If you give away just one card a day, you will have given out 365 cards in a year or about 250 if you only do it only on weekdays. If just one in ten percent (10%) follow up and contact you, that's between 25-36 new clients a year. That's not a bad start. If you retain 75% of them as clients, that would be 18-27 new clients who became regular practice members. If you see them just once a week for a single session and you charge $100. per hour or session, that's $93,600. gross on the low side and $135,000. gross on the high side annually. And don't forget, if you have 18 new consistent clients and you work a five day work week, you'll take up close to 20 hours of time just working on them. That's four hours of your day, so it adds up considerably.

If you make it your goal to give away 6 cards a day, you will have given out nearly 2,000 cards in a year. If you take an even more conservative estimate that only 5% of those who receive your card will respond and make an appointment, you will still have nearly 100 new clients within the first year. If you can handle the volume, that's enough to establish an extremely successful practice. Of course, to get that many people to respond, it will take some time and attention to talk to them and show them that you're someone they can trust and want to work with. However, the more they recognize you as an expert in your field and a competent and compassionate person who can help them, the more people will make an appointment with you. Business cards can be the start of a very successful business, but you have to be willing to come out of yourself and give them away to everyone you meet. And remember, when you hand out your business card, give away **three** cards and tell them to give one to their friends. You'll be surprised at how many will actually follow through and do it and what a difference it will make to your practice. I know it sounds too simple to be true, but it works. Try it.

36.   Design and Create a Practice Brochure

A practice brochure is like a condensed hard copy of what you present on your website that you can give out to people as a tri-fold or a pamphlet. It explains what you do in your overall practice and gives people interested in your practice something to look at over a period of time. It also gives them something to read while they wait to see you. This is your opportunity to fully explain your purpose, state your intentions, display your motto and offer them those important testimonials of previous clients. Your brochure should be comprehensive, without being too exhaustive in its explanation. The photos and colors you choose are important to draw interest and give them a good feeling as they first pick it up and later as they look at it again. The specifics of color and graphics will depend upon each practitioner's viewpoint of how they see themselves and what they want to portray about their practice to their clients. You may opt for colored paper stock instead of four color printing to keep your costs down, but whatever you choose, it's important to make each client's initial impression positive and reflective of the fact that they are with a professional who practices professionally .

A photo or two is always helpful since it will help familiarize a prospective client with you before they meet you. It helps limits some of their initial anxiety in coming in to meet with you. Make sure you get a professional photograph taken of you.

The most important thing to include is testimonials in your brochure. These are the golden standard of advertising in any and all practices. Sprinkle them throughout the brochure so that everywhere they look, they'll find one to reinforce their commitment to making an appointment with you.

It is your choice as to whether you give a full name or initials of the person offering their testimonial, but you should always be sure to get a waiver from the person giving the testimonial ahead of time so that if anyone wants to speak directly with them, they may do so. If your testimonials are unsolicited, then let them know that as well. These are the most valuable type of testimonials.

When soliciting testimonials, ask those clients that are obviously satisfied with your services to give you as many as four (4) versions of their statement. Also, ask them if you can "mix-n-match" parts of them once you get them, as long as you let them see the final version before it's published anywhere. That's what most authors and publishers do and it works well.

37.   Design and Print Selective Brochures about Specific Issues

After you've designed your practice brochure, prepare similar brochures on individual topics or conditions you treat in your practice. This is especially important to expose new clients to other options available to them within your practice that they might not ever have discovered on their own. That way, it enhances the services you offer to your clients as well as opening up new opportunities for clients to take advantage of all the services you offer. Each brochure should have a different look to it, but still maintain a consistency with all others that says they are from the same practice. This can be done with a specially designed logo and/or motto so your clients and new people can easily see a thread throughout the different aspects of your practice. That way, when they're satisfied with one thing you've done for them, they'll be more prone to visit you for something else you do whenever a need arises for it.

I've found that it's best to use a "catch phrase" as the title for each new brochure. Make sure whatever it is you're using for a title is about the client's needs. In other words, what do you do that they need? Then answer the question with what you're offering. Make sure your initial title is posed as a question or a statement that the reader can identify with, such as "Migraines Making You Go Crazy?" or "Are You Stressed to the Max?" or "Stress Kills!"

These are things that people can easily identify with and become interested in quickly. It's a draw to grab their attention and attract them into picking it up and either reading it right away or taking it with them to read later. Or someone else reads it in their family once it gets left on a table or elsewhere. You'll be pleasantly surprised to receive many calls which come from those very brochures months and even years later when one surfaces on someone's desk as they're cleaning out and now have the time, intention and money to address that problem that's been with them too long.

Make sure each brochure includes testimonials from at least a few satisfied clients who are willing to allow you to use their names. They should be strategically placed so the tri-fold is opened, the first thing they see is a short phrase from a satisfied customer/client. That always opens the mental doorway to acceptance. Then, give them a short statement about what the issue is and how your particular healing modality can be effectively used to address it. You may even give a short case history of someone you helped if you have the space available. Case histories excite the readers' minds and increases their curiosity.

Always make sure to include a short biography of yourself so that people will immediately see what an expert you are. This will give them greater confidence in your abilities. If you've written a book or have some other product related to your practice, add them at the end so clients can see how in-depth your knowledge and interest is in that topic.

Most importantly, include all of your office's information including address, telephone number, fax number and your email address. Finish off this section by including your website address so they can immediately access more information about you and your practice and satisfy themselves about you and your abilities. In fact, make sure your website address is on everything you publish about yourself and your office. Also make sure there is a discount offer with a very short expiration time (not date) on your website's landing page for that advertisement so they'll be more prone to buy something or at least leave their email. See p. 100 for more details.

38.   Design Professional Looking Flyers for Specific Events

Every time you are going to hold a special event related to your office or for your practice, it's important to distribute a professional looking flyer that notifies everyone about it. Flyers aren't difficult to design, but they do take some time and attention. There are specific software programs that can help you design them already within your computer. Do a little research and you'll find them there or you can buy special programs that will take you step by step through the entire process to completion.

I suggest you incorporate a photograph and/or logo so that it draws people's interest.   Also, vary the font size and boldness so readers will maintain interest and read it to completion.

When writing a flyer, make sure to put a title on it that is in a larger font size (16-24) and a unique font so it will draw attention to it. Make the rest of the flyer a little larger (14-15) than you would ordinarily use. Many people may just be walking by your flyer and not have their glasses on to read it. If it the text is large enough, they'll be able to read it anyway.

Make sure to include all salient information in the flyer so they know:
- what the workshop/seminar or event is about;
- where it's going to be held;
- when it's going to take place; and
- how much its going to cost.

Always make sure to give them a contact number and tell them to make reservations ahead of time due to limited seating. Always make sure to get money paid in advance or many well-intentioned people who want to come may have something come up at the last minute and if they're not well and truly committed to your workshop, they'll jump to the next thing that interests them instead. If they have invested some money beforehand, then they will be more likely to show up or at least call and reschedule in advance.

You may also wish to consider making up three or four different flyer forms that you can then use as a template to use every time you're planning to do another event. That way, you don't have to re-invent the wheel each time you plan to do a program or workshop.

39.   Write Pamphlets About Each Modality You Use

By writing a pamphlet about every modality you use in your practice, you are giving prospective and established practice members the opportunity to read about what you've done in your practice with other clients, what different modalities you can use for different conditions and what you can do for them in the future. A pamphlet of this nature should be about 6-14 pages long. Make sure to include several case histories and testimonials that are different within each pamphlet since they make each one interesting and exciting to your clients.

When choosing a cover photograph for each type of pamphlet, make sure it looks interesting and elicits an emotion from the reader which has direct relevance to the contents of the pamphlet. You can use the back cover to explain more about you and what you do in your practice. These are great vehicles for long term acceptance by the public of what you do, since they tend to hang around the house and be picked up repeatedly and read by different people over time. It has been estimated that pamphlets like these can survive in a household for a few months to a few years with different people reading them at different times. That keeps your name and what you do in their consciousness for an extended period of time and that always leads to new clients. Don't underestimate the "staying power" and "drawing power" of a well written pamphlet.

Also, remember, everyone wants to go to a specialist because they think that they'll get the very best care by only seeing a specialist. If you are perceived as a generalist in your practice and you do a number of things exceptionally well, you can't very well be a specialist in most prospective people's minds.

By writing a different pamphlet about each of your "specialities" you are effectively becoming that "specialist" to the people who read that one pamphlet. Also, it is easier to write a pamphlet about a specific modality that you use or issue you address than to write a general type of pamphlet. Specialty pamphlets are invaluable to your clients who never knew you used certain modalities in your practice. Once they read your pamphlet on a specific area of interest, they will be alerted to your abilities and be better equipped to use them in the future.

40. Prepare a 30 Second "Elevator Talk" About What You Do

Wherever you go, you'll usually run into someone who asks you what you do for a living and is willing to listen to you for a short time, say, between 30 seconds to two minutes. A good example is in an elevator. Elevators are usually an uneasy place for most people. They stand near to each other and often don't know what to say or do. While it may sound a bit trite, if you want to break the silence, do it with a prepared talk about what you do. It is always best to practice ahead of time so you don't have to cast about trying to think of how to tell people about what you do. Write out your talk and hone it down until you can talk about the most salient points in under 2 minutes. Hold in reserve something extra for questions when time permits. Once you have your prepared speech down pat, practice it repeatedly in the mirror and perhaps even use a recorder so you know how it sounds. It will also be easier to critique yourself if you can hear yourself speaking. Make sure that your speech is short, complete, effective and interesting.

You'll be surprised at how many people will actually ask for your business card and follow-up at a later time if your talk is compelling and interesting to them. Don't underestimate this powerful opportunity to make new contacts. Don't limit yourself to just using it in elevators. Use it everywhere you go. Whether its waiting in a doctor's office, a cocktail party or waiting for a train, people are people and they love to hear a good story. Make your story a good one and watch the results you get.

41.   Establish a Testimonial Book for Your Office

Have a testimonial book in your office waiting area so that new (and established) clients can review comments from satisfied customers. Of course, it's important that you monitor what goes into this type of book since you only want good testimonials, but make sure its prominently displayed and available to everyone. This can be especially effective in easing new clients' fears and those who are still a little uneasy with alternative therapies or with you in particular. By viewing letters written by previous clients, you are helping them resolve their concerns and offering them peace of mind before their treatment. This can be invaluable since it will help them relax and accept your ministrations better than by just speaking with them in a pre-talk or initial interview alone.

When you make up a testimonial book, it's important to put the original handwritten letters into it in plastic sleeves or have them laminated so the letters can't be harmed through continuous use. If the handwriting isn't legible, add a typewritten version next to or below it so it can be more easily read. It's usually a good idea to include enough letters to show that you've received them, but not so many that it appears that you're bragging about yourself. Just include enough to get the job done and leave it at that. You'll be surprised at how well those letters will work.

42.   Offer Free Pens or Pencils to Clients

When clients come to see you, make pens/pencils available for them to take home. It keeps your name, website and phone number in front of them - over a long period of time. Whenever they use that pen, they see your name and it gives them a subtle reminder that whenever they need you, they can find your information at the tips of their fingers.

Make sure to put some pertinent words on the side of the pencil or pen (like your motto, etc.) so they will be urged to visit you regularly and often. Use a slogan that you use throughout your practice and repeat it on just about everything you offer to your clients. Remember, Home Depot, Lowes and just about every large corporation uses slogans and they spend millions of dollars publicizing them. Whey do they do it? Because it works. It can work for you too, no matter how small you are or how little you spend on your slogan, motto or design you repeatedly use. If your clients see them enough, it will anchor your name and your practice in their minds and that's what ultimately gets results.

43. Give Away Free Calenders Each Year

Again, it keeps your name and face in front of clients the entire year. Wallet-sized is actually the best. Put your phone number, address and email on the reverse side.

This is another idea that still works like a charm. Everyone needs a calender each year and the best ones are those that people carry around with them in their wallets. You know, those little plastic ones that they refer to from time to time. If your name and contact information is on the top, bottom and/or back of that little calender, they will always know where and how to find you when they need you. A nice photo of you or something beautiful is also a nice touch to give them a lift whenever they see it.

The same holds true of larger calenders. People often post their calender at the beginning of the year on a door, refrigerator or elsewhere so they can refer to it whenever they need to. That's why so many retailers, insurance companies, restaurants, etc., offer them to their customers. It works to keep your name in front of clients for a mere few cents is a small price for a big return in this case.

If you have the time and want to make your calender unique, you can take photographs throughout the year at special events or just during office hours of practice members and staff. Once you have the photos you can input them into a computer driven program and make up your own calender. You can find these calender offerings all over the internet and you can also buy your own programming to do it in your own office. However, its been our experience that its usually best to get the final product professionally produced so it looks artistic, crisp and professional. Remember, your clients are going to be looking at it all year long, so you want to give them something good to remember about you.

Again, make sure to use your practice's slogan or motto on the face of each page of the calender. That way, each time they look up a date, they simultaneously see your face and your slogan. Repeating that simple saying in their subconscious mind will bring in repeat business all year long.

44.   Inform Your Clients About Your Other Interests

By offering articles or information in your printed or emailed materials about something other than just what you do in your practice, you are helping your practice members learn more about you and who you are beyond your practice. You are widening their view of you and your practice which will give them more to relate to over time. If you enjoy fishing, hiking, kayaking, charitable work, sports or whatever suits you, it makes you more real and human to them and it helps eliminate resistance and resentment towards you as a professional.

Beyond that, if you are helping others outside of your practice who need help or you're working to help heal the world in some other fashion, you will be seen in a more philanthropic light by them. Of course, don't offer this information about yourself in a self-congratulatory way or it will simply look like another egotistical professional showing off. Instead, offer news, information and assistance to those in need selflessly and openly and watch how those that know about it start to see you differently.

It has also been my experience that by offering help to others, clients respond better than just coming to you for help for themselves. It displays an overall concern for one's fellow man/woman and that gives you the moral high ground and people like and respect that.

45.   Offer Something for Free. Twice. Then Charge a Fee.

We are all pretty much alike. We respond to free stuff more than any other single incentive. You've heard the old adage, "if it's free, it's for me," haven't you? If you are giving something away for free, make sure it is valuable enough to justify the recipient's interest or it will look cheap and detract from what you're giving them.

Remember the cardinal rule mentioned throughout this book: "What's in it for me?" That's always the question you have to answer before you do any marketing. What's in it for the prospective <u>client</u>? Once you answer that question, everything will start to fall into place.

As long as people get something for free up front, they're usually pretty happy about it and receptive to other things from you. After you have initially offered them something for free, then build even more rapport by offering them something else for free. Two freebies are better than one!

It is somewhat like chumming for game fish in the ocean. First you throw in some bait, hoping that when the larger fish see them they'll come over to eat. As they start to strike, you offer a few more fish, making them comfortable with you being there. Then, as they lose all their inhibitions and start to feast on dinner, you drop in a fish with a hook inside and when they eat that, they're hooked. The same thing is true with marketing. It may sound crass, but it's a proven method in marketing and you should at least know about it. Whether you choose to use it is up to you.

Offer people something small, but valuable enough that they will be interested in it. When you ask them to sign up on your website in order to get that first free thing from you, all you ask for is their name, email address and mailing address so you can send it to them. It is up to you whether you charge them for shipping and handling.

After they respond to that, offer them something else even more valuable for free. Now, if they've listened or read whatever you've sent them, they're starting to feel more comfortable with you and they've built up a level of trust in you since you've just sent them two things absolutely free and all you asked for in return was their name, address and email address. That's a very good deal in anyone's book.

Now, offer them something even more valuable at a reduced price - as long as they also order something from you for which they have to pay full price. Once they receive these items, you'll have established a client for life and retained someone new on your email list who is a motivated buyer. That's a very valuable addition for you and your practice because from then on, they will respond positively to just about anything you offer them as long as they find it interesting, useful and reasonably priced.

While this technique may sound very commercially oriented, you are actually giving them a number of things for free in good faith and only offering things they must pay for afterward. At the very least, you'll get their email address and be able to market to them in the future.

The only reason to do this is to break down their natural resistance to buying things from strangers for fear of being defrauded. Once you've initially removed that basic fear and resistance by delivering something of value to them in good faith and you've reinforced it with a second free gift, you're well on your way to establishing a sound relationship that will only burgeon as they continue to do business with you.

Gary Craig once explained at a live seminar that when he was in the business world, he would carefully research the people who he wanted to sell something to and then send them a $100 bill in a carefully worded letter. He never sent a check or just a single dollar bill as many others did. He sent a one hundred dollar bill and all he asked for in return was to be allowed a short period of time with them to explain what he had to offer. He claimed he always received a call allowing him to see them and that he was almost always successful in selling them a far more valuable product than the $100. he had spent. In fact, it worked like a charm. The difference was he was willing to make a substantial offer without strings attached just to get to speak to them. Keep that in mind when you're deciding what to offer for free. The quality of your initial offerings will make a big difference in the overall effectiveness of this method. However, once you overcome that basic resistance by providing quality products at a reasonable prices, the rest is easier.

46.   Discover or Invent New Places to Post Your Flyers

It is very important to get your flyers out to the general public when you're going to be doing a workshop, speaking engagement or seminar. However, everyone places their flyers on the grocery store bulletin board or in the Laundromat. In fact, so many people post their flyers in these spots, they've become more like "background noise" to most people and they've stopped reading most of them.

Instead, it is important for you to establish new places to post your professional looking flyers so that the right people see them and respond to them. Otherwise, they're almost worthless. Of course, make sure that your particular city, town or village doesn't have any prohibitions to posting them in the places you invent, but invent new ones nonetheless. Placing flyers in local bathrooms in fast food restaurants, gas stations, railroad stations, schools, colleges and bars might be a good start. In most of those places you'll find that as soon as the proprietor finds them in his or her place, they'll take them down, but at least they'll be up for awhile. Beyond that, you can post them in break areas of schools, factories, large retailers in bathroom areas or post them in malls or stadiums. Many court houses and post offices have bulletin boards where you can post flyers or notices. You can even place them on cars in parking lots (although this is illegal in many areas - make sure to check first before trying this one). You can hire people to personally hand then out on a busy corner or distribute them to various neighborhoods (without putting them in mailboxes, which is illegal) or you can make an arrangement with a newspaper to include them in their normal delivery for a somewhat larger cost. Anything you can think of is more than likely a good idea, since it will get your flyers out to the public and that's the idea of printing flyers. Be creative and watch what you come up with and how effective it can be.

NEWSPAPER, JOURNALS, MAGAZINES AND PRINT ADVERTISING

47.   Draft and Purchase Print Advertising

From a mainstream point of view, print advertising can be important for any practice, seminar and/or workshop. It is an effective way to get the word out to a broad audience about a new practice. However, you have to evaluate if it's the best way for you and your practice.

When you purchase print advertising, the price depends upon the distribution of the particular newspaper or magazine you want to use. You must look to see what their readership consists of and where it is located. In many instances, there are Pennysavers and Towne Cryer-type papers that are specifically directed at locations nearest and most beneficial to your office. That way, you don't have to buy advertising space in larger newspapers with little or no hope of recouping your investment because most of their readership will be too far away from you.

Before you actually place any advertising, make sure to ask these important questions of the salespeople who are trying to sell you an ad:
- What's your present distribution?
- When was it last estimated or counted?
- How many households subscribe?
- What's the count for a daily paper versus the Sunday edition?

Remember, they are trying to sell you advertising space and that's how they earn their living. If they don't have time to answer those questions, they obviously aren't interested enough in your business. Go elsewhere. Find someone who is sufficiently interested to give you answers to all your questions until you're fully satisfied. Otherwise, keep your money in your pocket and spend it in better places.

Once you find the right vehicle to advertise in, be consistent with it so that people reading the paper see your name repeatedly - day after day or month after month. Advertising is a long term investment that takes time to pay off. If they see your name and face repeatedly, it leads to familiarity and trust which usually leads to new clients. Make a commitment to a long term advertising campaign before you start. That way, you can anticipate what you're involved with and can establish an advertising budget beforehand. That's the only way it will pay off for you. Remember, if it didn't pay to advertise in print, you wouldn't see all those companies with their names in the newspapers and magazines over the years. But, it is a long term investment that takes time to adequately pay off.

With today's computers you can more than likely design your own advertising campaign and save yourself a lot of money. If you don't already have the necessary programs, it would be a good idea to purchase them and familiarize yourself with them so you get your ads exactly as you want them without any compromise.

48.   Prepare News Releases with Photographs Well in Advance

Whenever you intend to do a workshop/seminar or a speaking engagement, it's a good practice to alert the media so they can alert the people who may want to join your workshop - for free. Since the press is always looking for news to distribute (remember, that's their business and, by definition, news must always be fresh) if you make their research easier for them by providing information, they are usually more than happy to include it in their paper. It's a perfect symbiotic relationship.

To do a news release effectively, you'll need to know how to write one up and what to include to make it more interesting to an editor. Again, when you incorporate artwork, photos or graphics, it tweaks the attention of a reporter or editor because it makes for a more interesting article in their paper. If you are offering a news release or press release, it should be written up in a way that news writers are already familiar with so they'll see it as another piece of news for them to print as soon as they get it rather than having to dig through an introductory letter with a lot of extra thoughts and suggestions in it.

The way to do this is to familiarize yourself with the news articles in the local papers into which you want to put your articles. Usually, it comes down to the five W's: *who, what. when, where, and why*. Fill in the rest of the story to make it interesting and compelling. See how the professionals frame their topics, how they write them up succinctly to make them interesting to their readers and how they incorporate the five W's of the event. Once you see how they write up what they offer in their papers, you can emulate them before submitting anything new to them.

The most important thing is the title. Make sure it is attention grabbing and exciting. News people are susceptible to their own type of hype and since they like to use catch phrases and exciting headlines, it is best to emulate them and do the same.

Use your business stationery, which should look professional and well designed. Use capital letters for the headline and use a larger than normal font size (perhaps 16-22 points). Then write up the body of the release and end with a punchy type of ending that has a little excitement to it. Add a photograph separately once you're finished with it. It's always best to provide a good, crisp, clear photograph that publishers can use in their paper. That helps them make their release more interesting and it eliminates the process of them going out to shoot the photograph themselves. Black and white works best, but a good crisp color print will do the trick if the content is interesting. Attach any photograph with a paper clip so it doesn't fall off, but don't use a staple because that can often make the photo tear when it is taken off the paper if the reporter or clerk is in a hurry.

Here is a sample you can use:

NEWS RELEASE -
FOR IMMEDIATE RELEASE
July 9, 2008
Hempstead, New York

EMOTIONAL FREEDOM TECHNIQUE FIRST TIME DEMONSTRATED ON LONG ISLAND

THE MOST POTENT AND EFFECTIVE HEALING TECHNIQUE KNOWN TODAY IS GAINING WORLDWIDE ACCLAIM AT AN AMAZING PACE. IT WILL BE PUBLICLY DEMONSTRATED ON LONG ISLAND FOR THE FIRST TIME.

Emotional Freedom Technique uses acupressure and focused attention to obtain profound results for people suffering from everything from emotional pain to chronic physical pain. For the first time on Long Island, the Center for Inner Healing is offering a Free opportunity to experience this incredible healing technique at an open house to be held at

> 175 West Old Country Road
> Hicksville, New York 11801
> on March 24, 2008 from 7-9 P.M.

This technique is suitable for anyone of any age and works exceptionally well on just about any problem or issue.

The evening will feature Theodore W. Robinson and Maria Kramer-Robinson. They have both been practicing EFT for more than 10 years and are very knowledgeable and effective in what they do for others.

They are both known for their insights and perception which help others find their way in the emotional morass in which most people find themselves caught.

EFT is on the cutting edge of healing today and is sweeping the world with its effectiveness. Many people experience"One Minute Miracles" since they actually resolve some of their deepest issues in an extremely short period of time.

The evening will consist of a short teaching program and then the Robinsons will conduct mini-sessions for those in attendance.

One person who recently had a private EFT session after taking the course had this to say:

"The private EFT sessions with Ted were invaluable to me as I was going through the most intense emotional turmoil in my life. After one session with Ted, I was able to function calmly and effectively in my daily life in a way that was impossible before to the session. I am so grateful." - Jana DeLury

Don't miss this opportunity to experience Emotional Freedom Technique. It is changing the world.

This is just a short example of what a press release can look like. Of course, this is just what my wife and I have used, you may make yours up to fit whatever it is you want the press to print. Make it specific and interesting. Remember to get your headline right. Try a few versions until you get the one that grabs the reader and holds their attention.

Remember, they are looking for news every day but if you provide it to them sufficiently in advance (2-3 weeks for newspapers) of your event date, they are more likely to print it. Don't get too hung up on doing it exactly right. They're probably going to change it anyway. Just make sure to do it, get it to them in plenty of time and watch the results.

Another thing you need to do is to make a follow-up phone call and/or send an email to the news room to which you sent your press release so they know you're more than just a packet of papers being sent to all the newspapers. You'll only get about two-three minutes of their time on the phone (they're busy too), so make it short and sweet. Don't make a lot of small talk. Just get across to them who you are and remind them that you sent them a press release that has a time limit for getting it into their paper. Make sure to follow-up with a short email to verify you just spoke with them. That keeps you and your press release in the forefront of their mind and that's what ultimately will get the job done. Remember, the entire purpose is to get the public to read about you, your practice and whatever it is you're promoting. And to do it for **free**! This is one of the most effective ways to accomplish it.

49.   Prepare Articles for Inclusion in Professional Journals

Nothing confirms your professional status better than the inclusion of an article written by you in a professional Journal. Journals are the vehicle within which professionals share information and discoveries with one another and launch controversial questions within their fields of interest as well as to the general public. Often, professional Journals are peer reviewed by members of committees that have to approve the content before they will allow it to be published under their auspices and that's what makes it so impressive to the rest of the professional world. In effect, a number of peers are standing behind the article to one degree or another and that helps justify its contents and support the position taken within it. This is a very important type of publishing to consider for yourself because once your article is accepted for publication, it will be in the public forum forever with your name attached to it. This can bring great benefits to you when submitting a *curriculum vitae* or resume to organizations or if potential clients wish to look you up ahead of time, it reflects well upon you. Professional articles also get picked up by Google and other search engines, so it improves your overall standing on the Internet as well.

If you wish to offer an article for inclusion into a peer reviewed Journal, you will first have to determine which Journal you want to be included in. My first suggestion is you do a word search on "peer-reviewed journals" or "alternative health care journals" or whatever best describes your field of interest and see what comes up. If you believe you have some new information to offer or a new approach that might be able to be included in a medical/psychological/holistic, etc. type of journal, then do a word search for that and submit it to them for consideration. Send them off to the editor or publisher and they will then tell you whether they are interested enough to pass it along to their review staff. If they are interested and it gets to be reviewed, don't be surprised if it is sent back to you for revisions repeatedly. This is not unusual, since essentially, once they publish it, their entire peer review group is standing behind your theory or practice and they want to make sure they are truly in keeping with it and everything it concludes before they sign off on it. If this happens, it can take a considerable amount of time to get it finalized, but it is well worth it when it finally goes to print. This is exactly where most of the great scientific and other discoveries are initially reported and the press and community at large is constantly scanning these for breakthroughs and reporting on them.

50.   Offer a Coupon in Local Advertisements

There are many local advertising magazines and newspapers that are free because they are fully funded by advertisers who are seeking business. Many of them are slick, full-color and have a very professional look to them. If you're going to use this type of vehicle for spreading the word about your practice, make sure that it is done as professionally as possible since most of the advertisers are retailers trying to get people to visit their stores and you don't want to look cheap or unprofessional in your advertising. Make sure you're going to place your advertising in the right vehicle for what you want to accomplish. To do that, make sure to review all available magazines and newspapers in your area ahead of time and only advertise in the ones you feel the most comfortable.

Next, once you are satisfied that this is the right place for you to advertise, include a coupon that expires within a certain short period of time. That way, the reader is prompted to take action within that time frame.

Otherwise, although they may have every intention of calling you for an appointment, as every minute or day ticks by after they've seen your ad, there is less and less likelihood that it will ever get done. The idea is to get the reader to take an immediate step to contact you even if it means giving them a coupon that will cost you a bit of money in the bargain. It is well worth it because without it, they may never call at all. Once they see you and experience your abilities, they'll be motivated to come back and that's when you make up for anything lost in the coupon.

The same thing holds true for using a coupon on your website. If anyone visits your website and doesn't take immediate action to accomplish something, then you've effectively lost them for good. It is always better to offer them a coupon that expires within a short period of time, such as <u>that</u> day. Otherwise, they lose interest or simply forget and neither one works to your benefit - or theirs. But that's the nature of most people and coupons is one quick way to remedy the situation.

51.   Write Editorials for Your Local Newspaper or Magazines

By writing letters to the editor or by doing visiting editorial pieces for your local newspaper and/or magazines, you'll be further solidifying your public image as an expert in the field in which you are commenting. Of course, it is vastly important that you only comment upon those issues in which you are an expert. That way, if anyone ever questions your opinion, you have a legitimate reason for offering it and you can back it up with your experience and credentials. By writing in, you are offering something of value to the community. Of course, make certain that whatever you write is not allowed to be edited without your express permission so it doesn't become anything other than precisely what you wrote. Make sure that anything you write is spell checked twice and reviewed by somebody else for grammatical errors before you send it in. Make sure your article makes sense when read by the typical reader and not just by other people in your field of expertise. You certainly don't want to write something for everyone to see if it doesn't reflect well upon you and your reputation. If your article is well written, then make sure to share it with the world and particularly your local community. There are a lot of people out there and you can be sure many of them will read what you write, whether you know about it or not. At the very least, it will spread your name across a large audience.

MARKETING THROUGH EMAIL

52.   Establish an Email List

This is probably the most important suggestion you can adopt to market your practice at the outset and throughout your career. Your email list can be used to make new offers to old clients or people who are already interested in you and what you do. Your existing clients - even if they haven't seen you in a long time - are already on your side and open to you and what you offer. This is far better than doing any general advertising because none of the people who see a general advertisement know you or trust you yet. Your email list already does both.

Your email list should be comprised of everyone you know and everyone who ever contacted you. Why? Because everyone you meet or speak to is evaluating you and deciding whether they think you have some ability or knowledge (expertise) that would be useful to them in the future. If they've contacted you, it can be assumed they are interested in you and what you do. By keeping in touch with them, you keep your name in front of them and that keeps you in their consciousness. Whenever they have a need your services, they will be more likely to think of you and how you can help them rather than someone else. This is a long term commitment, but it's the life blood of your practice and it's well worth the effort. Once they're on your list, it takes very little effort to keep them there.

Beyond that, email is presently free or almost free and that means, other than for the time and expense of preparing new emails, they can go out to as many people as you like for very little money. By comparison, paper mailings (letters and postcards) and other forms of advertising are far more expensive.

The people on your email list have already evidenced some interest in you and that means that you are effectively "target marketing" them. Your rate of success are far better using targeted marketing than blanket advertising such as ads in newspapers, radio and TV. In those type of forums they rely upon selling to a smaller percentage of a much larger audience.

With email, the reverse is true. You can send to a far smaller number of recipients and you'll usually get a higher percentage of purchasers. One thing to remember - as you increase the number of interested people on your email list, you will eventually get a far higher rate of return than from any other form of advertising. If you keep building your list, you'll find that your practice will keep growing with it. Almost everything you initially do with a new person should be geared to getting their email address onto your list and then working with it from there.

Once you have your email list initially in place, it's time to use it to keep in touch on a regular basis. This can be a valuable means of maintaining and then improving your image with your clients/patients/customers. As you'll see in other parts of this book, announcements, newsletters, discounts, special dates and events and a host of other important and mundane things can be shared with your practice members quickly, easily and cheaply through email. By the way, notice I said "practice members." That's because it's my contention that everyone of those people who use your services are not only clients but members of your practice. They have something to say about how your practice is conducted and where it's going. You'll want to be responsive to their needs and desires so it is important that you listen to them and what they want and that will help mold your practice.

53.   Write an Email Newsletter Regularly

Writing a regular newsletter is an important adjunct to the rest of your practice since it keeps you and your practice in your client's minds. As mentioned before, "content is king" on the Internet so your newsletter must have new content on a regular basis to keep people interested in reading it. In fact, the more interesting and unique the content, the more they'll look forward to reading it, which will keep them engaged and connected with you. It will also help them get to know you better and feel more comfortable with you as time progresses.

Make your articles pertinent to whatever you do within your practice. Show people what others are doing in your practice by offering some case histories - without names, of course, and with that client's prior permission, even if you've changed the name on the story. Make sure to state that the client gave their permission for you to include their story so nobody worries that whatever they say to you could wind up in your newsletter later. This is important for them to know ahead of time so they'll trust you implicitly and feel comfortable being open about their problem or issue.

Vary what you put into your newsletter. Perhaps a menu, poem, quote or motto and then an article or two. Don't make your newsletter too long or most of it won't get read. Make one article light and airy and the other one more substantial and interesting. That way, there's a little in there for everyone and they get to learn something if they want to or just scan it for general interest and move on. It is actually a good idea to vary the length and format of each newsletter so your readers don't get attached to only one type of newsletter coming from you. And don't get attached to whether anyone is reading your newsletter. You'll often discover over the years that a lot more people are reading it then you'd suspect. They may mention it to you when you least expect it. Remember, your articles keep you in their minds and that's exactly where you want to be when they finally need your services. That's one reason you give them a few case histories from time to time, so they can see what you can do for people and they can relate to it if they should ever feel that way themselves and need help.

One thing, <u>don't call them newsletters</u> if you can help it. Or, if you do, use another name with it so that it softens the "N" word. We call ours "About You" because it is intended to be about the reader and what we can do for them in our practice. People are often inundated with newsletters, many of which aren't all that good and they effectively become spam to many people. It's your job to make what you send out interesting enough that people look forward to receiving it, reading it and getting something out of it. It can be an invaluable asset to your practice. It is an investment of time, but in my opinion, a worthy one.

When you start off, you can use your email alone to send out your newsletters. However, make certain that you only use Blind Carbon Copies (BCC) rather than just sending out Carbon Copies (CC). That way, nobody else can access your email list and use it to send their email to your list. This situation will automatically be different if and when you use an email communications service like the one we use in our office. We use ConstantContact.com which is an Internet service that use to send out our newsletters and keep track of them for us. The cost is minimal and the service is great. All we have to do is access our account, choose a format for our newsletter (we try to change it regularly to keep our readers interested) and fill in the format with content. Some formats allow for photographs or other graphics, while others don't. Some give you two columns and others just one. There are hundreds to choose from and it allows you many options so you can keep your newsletter interesting. I suggest you consider using such a service since it makes it easier to put together your email and once its sent out, they'll also keep you informed of the status of your mailing list. If you gain or lose any readers, you'll know about it each month. This helps to keep you informed of what drives your readers actions and allows you to modify what you do each time you send out another newsletter. There are other email services available on the Internet. You can research what each one offers and find the perfect match for your needs.

Again, if you want to send out a newsletter but don't yet know how to go about it, here are a few ideas to help you get started or to improve what you've been doing so far. First, content is king on the Internet. If you're a good writer, then write your own articles. Write them from your own perspective so that your readers will realize who you are and what you're about. If you don't feel comfortable writing your own articles, there are a lot of websites on the Internet that offer free or for fee articles you can draw from. Again, simply go to any search engine and type in "articles" or "free articles" and they'll pop up for you. You can then review their offerings and choose the article that impresses you and write up smaller items around that article. The same thing goes for saying, quotes and mottos. You can find them on many sites and once you find a quote you like, you can include it in your newsletter to set the tone of that letter. Make sure to include the author's name so they get the credit for their quote. Most of the time that should avoid any potential copyright problems, but check with the website where you found them to make sure if you have a question about it.

As for including photographs in your newsletter, I find that they add balance and interest to any newsletter, so I almost always include at least one photograph beyond a photo of myself and/or my wife. I almost always include a photo of one or both of us just to keep our face in our reader's view. That way, we don't just become a faceless author. We're actually people writing to them, we don't want anyone to forget that fact. Photos work well to keep you connected with them.

To find other photographs, there are various types of services on the Internet from which you can gather photos that interest and inspire you. We use Shutterstock.com which is a subscription type of service that costs a set fee for 30 days of access to millions of photographs. Presently you can download 25 photos per day for 30 days for under $200.00, however, those amounts are sure to change with the passage of time. There are a number of such services on the Internet and there are also free download services. Again, just type in "copyright or royalty free photos" or "free photos" into any good search engine and you'll gain access to quite a few of them. They all have different parameters for usage and most of them have different usage rules so that if you're going to use an image for more than a certain amount of printings, then you'll have to pay a higher royalty fee. However, if you're just using the photos for a limited size newsletter list, the normal royalty limitations shouldn't effect you. As usual, always check their limitations before making your own decision as to which one to use since it can make a difference if you wind up using an image and suddenly have a blockbuster book on your hands and as the author you've used one of their images for your cover design.

In conclusion, always make your newsletters as interesting and varied as you can so your readers continue to read them. Include a photograph or two and something a little different than most others do and you'll find your readership will keep you in their minds regularly and that will make a difference in your practice.

MARKETING THROUGH THE INTERNET

54.   Design and Establish a Website for Your Practice

If you're computer savvy at all, by now you know it's imperative that you have a website of your own for your practice. If you're not completely computer literate yet, then it's high time you hire somebody to build you a site or teach you how. Building your website doesn't have to be done exclusively by you. You can hire individuals and/or firms to build and maintain your site for you, but it would be best to have someone "in-house" who is familiar with website design and updating so that it gets done regularly and without additional travel expenses. However, even that can be eliminated these days by doing the entire process over the Internet between you and any expert you hire.

While establishing a website can be a tremendous amount of work, it is a direct reflection of you and your practice on the Internet and is an absolute necessity today. The Internet is international in its scope and allows anyone from around the world to find and communicate with you instantly. I've had people from as far away as Dubai contact me and come to New York for classes just because of my website and their ability to access it from their own home in the Middle East. Make sure any website you build looks as professional, yet inviting, as possible.

The first thing you want to do is determine your primary purpose of establishing a website. Do you want to sell something or offer a service? Or both? Make that decision before you even call a webmaster to design your site. That way, you'll have an idea of how you will transform an empty computer screen into a fascinating and dynamic entree to you and your practice for visitors.

To help you make the basic decision, visit as many websites in your field of interest as you can and see what it is you like and don't like about them.

- What grabs your attention the most?
- What turns you off about the site?
- Was there anything in particular that made you take action and order something from a site?
- What was it?
- Did you take action at all? And if not, why not?
- Was the site easy to navigate (move about)?
- Was it easy or difficult to find things on it?
- Was the site clean looking and streamlined or cluttered and difficult to follow?
- What did you like most about the site?

Make notes on all of these questions and then pick out and note five websites that caught and maintained your attention and list them. Then, when you meet with your webmaster or when you start to design the site yourself, you'll have various examples of what you liked the most and what features you want on your own website.

The use of color and design are especially important to the person who first visits your website to see what you and your practice are all about. Next, is content. However, just like everything else on the Internet, content is the most important aspect of any site. If you have interesting and engaging content on your site, it tells the viewer that you have something interesting to offer them and they will usually decide they would like to learn more from you. If they like what they see and read, it's their first step toward getting them in touch with you and making an appointment for treatment or purchasing a product from you.

It's at that very moment that your website must do <u>its most important job</u>. Your website must assure that the visitor is sufficiently impressed with you and your practice that they will either contact you, buy something from your site or at the very least, leave their email address with you. Any one of these gets the ball rolling to taking further steps towards transforming them into practice members. No matter what else it does, your site must get each new visitor to take some sort of action before they click onto another site or leave the Internet. If you accomplish that, you've got a successful website.

One way to have visitors take action is to offer something for free or at an obvious deep discount. You can offer a free health evaluation, a CD or MP-3 from a past workshop, a free download from your website or almost anything that may interest them and will get them to click on that spot that asked them for their email address. Whatever it is you offer, make sure that you follow-up with them by first auto-responding within moments of taking their order. This gives them a message that you received their order, thank them for it and assure them they will receive their order within a short time. Auto-responders are programs that usually come with your email program. All it takes is to set your automatic message back to whoever responds to your website. Then, if they show other interest, make sure you get back to them quickly again to make an appointment with them. That way, you'll keep whatever momentum you've started by having them visit your website and move them towards becoming a practice member or a regular purchaser of your products.

There is much more you can do using your website, which will be discussed in other areas, but the first thing to do is get a good basic web site online and then work to update and improve it over time. Another thing to remember is that once you have a website, it's important that you update the content regularly. That way, visitors will be interested in returning at a later time which is exactly how you establish rapport with them and build your practice.

55.   Offer an Immediate Discount on Your Website

When people find your website, statistically they'll only stay on it for about 90 seconds unless there is something compelling to keep them there. So, within that 90 seconds, you must give them an obvious incentive to decide to do something about seeing you, calling you, writing you or leaving their email behind so that you to can respond to them.   If your site doesn't accomplish that task within that first 90 seconds, then you might just as well not be on the Internet. You're effectively wasting your time and money.

The key to getting most people to do one of those things is to "Make Them an Offer They Can't Refuse" or "An Offer That's Too Good To Be True" so they almost have to take you up on it. One of the best is to give them an "electronic coupon" for a limited period of time (like before they leave that web page or your site - or within 20 minutes or an hour - your choice) that saves them money. That offer can be just about anything that gets them to take action.

One suggestion is to give them a discount on something that looks good and has value to it. You may wish to offer them a 25-50% discount on an ebook or one of your services if they contact you before leaving the site. Or offer them a free download of something that you're offering for sale on your site so they can see you're offering a legitimate discount. Make sure the coupon is noticeable and prominently placed somewhere close to their "landing point" on each page of your website given whatever word they searched for that got them to your site. A "landing point" is where someone "lands" when they reach your site after searching for it on a search engine. It is determined by them clicking on certain words when they do a search and their search brings them to your site. This occurs when you post what are called "meta-tags" on each page of your website. "Meta-tags" are simply descriptive words representing the content on each page. For instance, we have a web page called "Emotional Freedom Technique" for which we've posted meta-tags of Emotional Freedom Technique, EFT, healing, emotional healing, issues, resolution, holistic, acupressure and a number of others that describe what Emotional Freedom Technique is all about. That way, when someone types in the word "EFT" into a search engine, that web page will show up and the person will "land" on a particular area of that page that has the acronym "EFT" written there. That's the landing point and it is important to remember where it is so you can place one of your coupons at that point. Otherwise, the reader may never get to the point of finding your coupon within the normal ninety seconds they'll spend there before leaving your site.

Also, make sure to give them a spot on your home page and every other web page on your site to sign up for a free newsletter so you get their email address. That is perhaps the most important reason for doing any of this because once you have their email address, you can make all kinds of offerings to them in the future and keep in touch with them over time. Also, always make sure you have an auto-responder send them a message as soon as they do anything on your website from signing up for your newsletter to purchasing something. That way, they're assured they've made a connection with you.

Once they like what you have to offer on your site and they like whatever it is they've purchased from you, you've got a satisfied customer and a relationship that is priceless. Once they trust you, it is much easier to maintain that relationship and provide them with more products and services over time and that is usually the primary purpose of having a website in the first place.

56.   Draft and Purchase "Pay-Per-Click" Advertising

First, in case you're not yet fully familiar with them, search engines help you find information on the Internet by matching the word or words you use wherever they are located on the Internet. Pay-Per-Click advertising on search engines is one of the most effective ways to advertise. It is the best way to reach people who are motivated to purchase exactly what you're offering and that's an important distinction. They are already searching the Internet for something they want and it's also what you're offering. What could be better? They type in the most descriptive words they can think of about whatever it is they're looking for and then the search engine provides a match on their computer screen. If your name is one of the top three that pop up, there's a very good likelihood that they'll click on it and the next thing you know, they'll be visiting your website and reading all about you and what you have to offer them. In fact, they'll actually "land" on the very page that has the words they've been searching for so they don't have to travel all over your website to find it once they get there. The reason Pay-Per-Click advertising is so compelling is because it makes it easy for the searcher to find you. Here's how the advertising system works:

When someone types in a word for which they're searching, that word will be searched for by the search engine and everything containing that word will show up on the results page in the search engine. However, that word, or series of words, carry a value to them based upon how much someone has offered to pay to be the first one at the top of the list of results found on the search engine. In other words, there's an auction for each search word and whoever bids the highest amount for that word becomes the one that gets placed highest on the page. If someone outbids your bid, then they wind up in the first place on the page. Remember, that first position can be a very important place since so many people are only interested in results on the Internet and they want to do things quickly. If it's easiest to click on the first name that pops up, so be it. That's what they'll do. That' why this type of advertising is so compelling and valuable to most advertisers.

I've spoken to business people who have told me that Pay-Per-Click has made their entire business what it is and without it, they wouldn't have 1/10 of the business they have now. They are willing to pay almost any price for those initial clicks which provide contacts directly to their website because they know that once they have attracted new people to their site, they will make them an offer they usually won't refuse. They may offer a discount coupon if they immediately buy something, a free CD, a free downloadable article, free pamphlet or any number of other incentives to get them to do business with them the first time. After that, if the product and/or work done is satisfactory to the customer, they have more than likely established a long term customer or client and then its almost easy to sell them anything that has value and a reasonable price.

Customers and clients don't easily change people with whom they do business with. It takes them time and effort to interview a new business operator or professional and they never know if the next one will be as good as the last. Instead, once they establish rapport with someone by successfully doing business with them, even one time, they usually prefer to stay with them than jump around to another unknown website. The initial establishment of a business relationship is a very important step and once built, it is not easily disturbed.

Pay-Per-Click is a very important way to establish a new business relationship at a very reasonable cost. You can't beat the business model. That's why Google is already such a valuable company and promises to be even more valuable as time goes by. If you haven't yet looked into this option, make sure you do in the very near future. You won't regret it.

57.   Invest in Other Forms of Paid Internet Advertising

There are a number of other forms of paid advertising on the Internet which include the use of banners at the top and bottom of various web pages. To invest in banner advertising you'll first want to find which websites or other locations you think your prospective clients will also be visiting. Otherwise, you'll be spending money to advertise when there are few, if any, prospects reading your ad. To do that, you can visit any good search engine and enter the words "advertising results on websites" or similar words. You should receive answers that will not only give you the number of visitors, but a full profile of them. The profile should include what they normally buy or use from that website and what they are looking for from it. Once you've evaluated the profiles and found them to be compatible with your purpose, then it's a wise move to advertise on that site.

To place a banner advertisement, the first thing you'll want to do is determine which site you would most like to advertise on and then contact the site webmaster which is the person in charge of the site. Inquire as to their ability and interest in mounting a banner on the top or bottom of their home page (opening page) or on another landing page (where most visitors land when they have asked a specific question that relates to what you're interested in). If they are interested, then it's time to see what they know about it and how much they want to run your banner ad per month or longer. The longer you agree to run your ad, the less the amount you should pay because they are then establishing a long-term relationship with you, they don't have to sell any advertising to anyone else during that entire time. That takes a big burden off them and that makes it cheaper for you to take on such an ad. Of course, you'll usually only take a limited time period so you can monitor the results you get with your ad and determine whether you want to do more. If so, that's when you'll want to negotiate a better figure for yourself depending upon how long you agree to advertise.

To post a banner ad the website will ordinarily provide the necessary software to fill in the information you wish to convey. However, if you really want to display something that will make a real difference which results in new clients, then you'll ordinarily have to develop your own advertising content and find the right software to accommodate it. It is normally best to hire a professional web designer to accomplish such work, however, you can also find additional information and advertising videos about how to specifically do banner advertising on YouTube.com under Banner Advertising.

58.   Write an Internet "Blog"

A blog is a website maintained by a person or a business entity where they can post opinions, comments, notices, videos, music or just about anything else you want on the Internet through your own portal. Each type of blog has a different nickname to it: a micro blog has only very short posts on it; a video blog is called a vlog; a music blog is called an MP3 blog; a podcast site in which simple audio is disseminated is effectively a blog.

However, most blogs are like diaries in which people can post their ideas, thoughts and commentaries to the world. One good reason for maintaining a blog is because the Internet (cyberspace) is a space that is almost as vast as the Universe itself. It's easy to get lost in it and nobody will ever find you unless you take the necessary steps to be found. As mentioned before, the best way is to be noticed by the search engines. Their primary purpose is to discover you and your website by searching the entire Net to see if your name shows up anywhere, but even more important is how often it shows up. Since a blog is a website, it is a place where you can get your name out to the world and those all-important search engines.

When you start a text driven blog (which basically is like a public diary) and post to it regularly on the Internet, it represents one more place that those search engines can readily find you and it adds to your overall search engine rating. This is one reason why its important to have a blog. The reason a blog is similar to a diary is that it can take any form you want it to take, but usually you write your thoughts and feelings on things that effect you, your practice, your profession and the world and send it out into cyberspace for everyone else to read it.

As you disseminate your writing to the world, readers have the chance (if you choose to allow a response on your blog) to respond to your writing. This can be a good option to choose because the search engines are also looking at all of the names of the people who are responding as well and if they show up on your blog, then that will lead the search engines to mention your blog. Your search ratings go even higher and it becomes easier to find you through yet another connection on the Internet.

The reasons the standings are so important is because most people searching for something or someone on the Net are impatient and the first few names that pop up after entering a word search is usually what they click on and review before making their choice of who they ultimately want to connect with. If you show up in one of the top six placements on a particular search you have a much better opportunity to be clicked on and contacted by a searcher. By being mentioned in more and more Internet websites and search engines you are more likely to organically show up higher in the ratings.

Blogs also give you the benefit of having a forum from which to express your views about just about anything you wish. It is especially useful if you talk about your profession and/or practice so that others who have the same interests will be more prone to finding and reading your blog and that only further improves your image in the world. If they respond to your comments, so much the better.

The real key to getting your blog out to the world is to post it on any number of blog forums or placement sites. To find them, simply type in "blog directory", "blog forum", "blog" or other similar words into any search engine. Google even has its own blog search facility. You may post your blog on any blog list (some have fees and some are free) and before long responders will be writing their comments on your blog and you'll get noticed and mentioned on Google and elsewhere more often than you ever expected. Blogging can be fun and fulfilling if you don't take it all too seriously. It can also be used effectively in expanding your practice if it's effectively used.

59.   Offer to Write Articles for Inclusion in Other Newsletters

Content, and especially, new content, is the name of the game on the Internet. If your website and/or newsletters don't have new content, they become old and stale quickly as far as most Internet readers are concerned. There is so much to look at and read on the Internet that anything that has been seen once is now old and not worthy of a second review. Newsletter writers are always looking for new content to fill their newsletters.

Once you've gotten used to writing articles for your own newsletter, you may find that you have extra articles that you want to offer to others for inclusion in their newsletters. Remember, not everyone is good at writing and they want to include new content as much as they can in their newsletters. There is a great demand for new articles all the time.

If you offer them an article they can use in their newsletter that doesn't conflict or compete with them or their practice, they're more than likely to use it. You also get the benefit of being published online and search engines count that for you in their exposure numbers for your name. It's a win-win for both of you.

When you offer your articles to others, make sure you only do it if they are willing to put your contact information at the end of your article. That way, if someone likes what you wrote, they'll know who you are, where you are and how to find you. This will often lead to new clients and an expansion of your practice.

Another thing to consider when offering your articles for publication in others' newsletters is that they also reciprocate or link their website back to your website in return for using your article.

60.   Offer Your New Articles to Free or Paid Articles Websites

As mentioned numerous times before, content is king on the Internet. Have you read this before somewhere? Since every website needs to upgrade and update their content on a regular basis, every site must gather or write new articles constantly. When they can't write them, there are websites that offer new articles for free and for fees. This is where you come in. If you write well and people like what you write, then you have a built in audience who may very well be willing to purchase your articles.

Once you write a new article, you can offer it to websites that you know are always looking for new stuff to publish on their website or you may wish to offer them to those websites that list articles that are offered to others on the Internet for publication. There are many websites offering free articles for publication on the Internet and there are websites that offer articles for fees for using. Either way, it gives you greater exposure and gets your name out to many, many people without any additional effort on your part. Once your article is posted on these centralized websites, many people will visit them and some will want to use your article or articles if they are interesting and insightful. Some may actually contact you directly and seek to hire you to write for them in the future. No matter what happens, you're already ahead of the game just by posting your articles on those sites and getting them published.

Just the fact that your name and articles are being posted on other websites will also inure to your benefit as far as the search engines are concerned. In fact, the more articles that are published on more websites, the better your reputation and standing on those search engines will be. So post as many articles as you can on those websites and watch how your standing improves over time. Your professional standing will also improve as you publish more articles and you just may make some money in the bargain.

The websites can be found on Google, Yahoo or any good search engine by typing in "Internet articles", "free articles", etc. Some examples of these type of websites that carry articles with new content are:

articlecity.com
articlegeek.com
articleauthors.net
website-articles.com
constant-content.com

61.   Offer to do Interviews on Web Radio Shows

Web radio may be new to many of you, but it is becoming a more commonplace event on the Internet. Once you are on such a show, it can get a loyal following and it can help you expose your name and expertise around the world. The primary purpose of Web radio is to play music, show videos and conduct interviews that are heard by anyone who accesses or subscribes to that particular website.

Web radio is listened to by many people who have no ability, due to their lack of proximity to radio stations, to listen to normal radio shows. For instance, if you live in New York, you can't listen to FM or AM radio being broadcast from California and vice versa. Of course, that also means that people in other areas of the world can't access radio stations from different continents. That is, until now! With web radio, people from all over the world can access any show on the web with no difficulty at all.

When people are interested in a particular topic and can't find it anywhere else, they can now turn to web radio. Most web radio web sites usually maintain an archive of past shows so that those who are interested can still listen to whatever you discuss for years to come. That means that one web radio appearance can lead to listeners years from now discovering you. Many web radio shows are now downloadable as podcasts. Many people may find your interview on iTunes or other sites and put it on their iPods and listen to it at a later time. It is a good media to utilize.

Web radio is still in its infancy and that makes it a lot easier to get invited onto it. Producers are looking harder to fill their time slots with interesting people. If you are interesting and can carry on an interview for a half hour or even a full hour and hold the audiences attention, you'll more than likely to be well received on a web radio show.

62.   Offer Yourself for Interviews on Web Television Shows

Everything just mentioned about web radio applies to web television. With the advent of iVideo iPods that display video, and telephones that have video access through them, it won't be long until everyone will want to see a video rather than just listen to radio. Also, with video, watchers get to see you and your body language as you speak about your topic. It makes it more interesting for them.

This is an especially good place to introduce your work if you do body work or healing touch of any type. Viewers can see exactly how you do the work you do and it will soften any innate resistance to using the methods you use. It will also lessen any resistance that they might otherwise have for your healing modality or technique. If you're especially handsome or beautiful, then video may also be the better vehicle for you to use.

One thing to remember with web television shows is that they're often a little easier to get invited onto since their producers are often looking harder to fill their time slot with interesting people than broadcast television shows. That's because there isn't yet as big a demand for Internet television, but as time goes on, this will change as well and Internet television will become more acceptable and in greater demand. If you are interesting and can carry on an interview for a short period, you'll likely be accepted on a web television show as a guest. Follow the same rules as listed for getting onto regular broadcast television and watch the fun begin.

63.   Offer Podcasts on Your Website and Elsewhere

Podcasts are a relatively new invention that came about as a result of iPods and their ability to download music and talks and then play them back to you whenever and wherever you wish. Podcasts can be offered free or by paid subscription, but before you can demand a subscription price, you need to build up a following first. That's usually done by offering your podcasts for free until you get enough people interested in what you have to say and how you have to say it to keep them coming back for more by paying you a subscription fee.

To make a podcast is fairly simple if you know a little about computers and recorders. They are comprised of an introduction over some music, the substance of the talk and then some closeout music to end it. This can all be done right on your computer and once you get the knack of doing it, it starts to become easier each time you do it.

You can find "canned" music on the Internet by going on any search engine and entering "royalty free music" and you'll find an amazing number of offerings that you can sample before buying. Just about any type of music you can imagine is available on the Internet for a fee and some of it is free. Just make sure that the terms of usage are that you can use it in making your own product and can sell it as often as you wish once its been made without having to pay the composer/producer any further royalties.

To actually record a podcast, you should have a digital recording device. We use an Edirol R09HR High Resolution Wave and MP3 Portable Recorder. It presently costs about $400. and has excellent sound quality even in difficult circumstances. It is also rechargeable. The Edirol uses a card for memory so you can easily download it into your computer for later editing. There are also other excellent portable digital recorders on the market put out by Sony and others, we just chose the Edirol because it was recommended to us as the best out there.

Once you have your program "in the can" and completely edited to your satisfaction, you can then place it online in any number of places to be seen by prospective purchasers. Starting with iTunes.com and moving to any number of podcast distributors like Podcast Alley, you'll find that people will order your podcasts and listen to them on their own schedule and then respond later to your subscription offers. In short, if the content interests them, they'll listen to it. If it really interests them, then they'll buy it.

Again, this gets your name out to the public and that always inures to your benefit. It builds your reputation and public image and that again leads to making you the obvious expert in your field of endeavor. It also leads to other speaking engagements, referrals and a host of other benefits that are mentioned throughout this book.

Podcasts are a great way to establish a regular audience and keep them returning for more visits to your web site. They offer a means by which listeners or viewers can access whatever content you've put on your site at any time after you've placed it there.

There are specific methods to follow if you want to make a podcast, however, they are more involved and technical than can be explained within the format of this book. In fact, there are entire books on the subject and there are a number of tutorials available to show you how to record a podcast and post it to various websites for free or for fee. The easiest and most convenient place to learn about it in more detail is to go onto YouTube.com and watch it. Just do a search on how to create a podcast and it will give you a list of videos to watch. You can also go on Google, Yahoo or any other search engine and again do a search on how to create a podcast. These are the best way to learn how to do podcasts and once you've done one, you're well on your way to doing more. Good luck with them.

64.   Post a Healing Session or Short Lecture on YouTube.com

If any part of your practice lends itself to being watched on video, then consider submitting a sample of what you do to YouTube.com or any other video sharing website.   In case you're not yet familiar with YouTube.com, it's a video submission site which will give you the opportunity to be seen worldwide by millions of people.   They already have over six million videos on their site and it is growing daily.   The posts that are already on YouTube about EFT and Hypnosis are impressive and are often compelling.   They connect you directly with the healer/practitioner as you watch them do their intricate work of healing which can be a big draw for many viewers.   YouTube is only a few years old and it is already growing exponentially.   There are also other video sites which you can find by using a search engine to search for"video sharing websites."   The only one I can personally vouch for so far is YouTube.com, but I'm sure others will benefit you as well.

As time goes by, more and more people will pick up on this trend and it will grow even larger.   If the video you post is compelling and word of mouth spreads, it can easily go to the top listing and that will get even more hits on your video.   You can also add a subscription button onto your video so that any time you offer a new video, viewers will automatically get to see it because it will show up on their computers automatically.

As every person watches you do your work (or "magic", as the case may be), they will make a judgment as to whether they like you and what you do.   If they do, they'll find your website noted on the video or posted next to it and they can then directly contact you.   And it's all for free - so far.   If you're going to post a video of yourself, make sure you do it professionally and do it well.   It makes a difference what people see of you and if they don't like you, they more than likely won't be back for a second look.   My suggestion is that you hire a professional videographer to shoot whatever you intend upon posting and have it edited professionally so it looks its very best.   That way, you look like the professional you want to portray - which is what the public perception should be.   Keep that impression alive in everything you do and you'll build your reputation and your practice as an expert.

Video is one of the most powerful mediums on the Internet. Its like watching television on your computer, but the difference is you're not watching commercialized television. Instead, you're watching regular people making their own videos and posting them on YouTube.com. Some of them can be very compelling, insightful and interesting.

One of the most effective things to do is shoot your own video about your practice or any part of your practice. Then, post your video on YouTube.com and link the opening page of your website to that particular video. That way, when someone new visits your site, they can watch you personally explain anything you want to them via that video. It's a great way to communicate and people are usually moved more readily with a video than anything else.

One of the best things about YouTube.com is you can post different videos for different web pages on your website. Each can apply to that page alone and give visitors different information. And you can change the video as easily as inserting a different link to a different video, so it makes it easy to change the look, feel and content of your website more easily than ever before.

Of course, you can also link to existing videos on YouTube.com on just about any topic you choose to talk about on your website and that again makes your site even more interesting to visitors which will bring them back to your site for more visits more often.

65.   Establish RSS Feeds to Your Website

RSS feeds are a simple way to make sure that visitors to your website will be aware of fresh content on it as soon as it arrives there. This eliminates the necessity of them typing in your website regularly to check on your website to see what's new and helps them stay current with whatever is going on with your site which keeps them in touch with you.

RSS mean "Really Simple Syndication" and is a means of web savvy people "subscribing" to your website, blog or any news group so that anytime something new comes out on the site they subscribe to, they'll be the first to get it.

In order to set up an RSS ability, you'll have to add an icon onto your website's home page so that anyone who wants to subscribe to your website will be able to click on the icon and type in their email address and that sets up their RSS connection. There is a generic icon which is orange and looks the same all the time and then there are specific icons that have names of things like "My Yahoo","Google", etc. which are consistently designed with the site they refer you to. All you have to do is click on that subscription button and the RSS starts to set itself up almost automatically.

For a detailed video explanation of how to set up an RSS feed and other associated information go to YouTube.com and search"RSS Feed."

RSS Feeds are the way of the future and they are a significant improvement on staying in touch with your readers on a regular basis.

66. Add Your Own and Others' YouTube.com or Similar Links to Your E-newsletters and Websites

Did you know you can add a specific video link to a particular video posted on YouTube.com into your newsletters? Well, you can. So if you like something you find on YouTube.com or a similarly video driven website and you want to share it with your practice members or everyone on your email list, all you do is go to YouTube.com or any other video web site and cut the specific Internet address of the video you like and paste it into your newsletter at the point that you're writing about it. When someone gets that link in a newsletter, it will jump over to YouTube and play that video for them directly. Not only does this add an element of action and interest, it shows you are savvy to new technology and have greater interests than just what you appear to be doing in your practice. It also gives people who see your newsletter something to talk to you about and open discussions into areas other than your practice. This sets up rapport more easily with your clients and they'll feel more comfortable with you.

You may prepare your own video offerings on YouTube and direct your readership to them so they can see other aspects of what you do in your practice. It is great for advertising and marketing you and your practice. But only do it if you look and act confident and professional.

Something to remember about using imported videos from another website like YouTube.com is the videos can be pulled from that site at any time without notice if the person that posts it wants to take it off or if the website believes it is inappropriate for any reason. So, before you add such a video post to anything you send out, make certain that the video is still posted on YouTube or any other site you refer them to and make sure there are no "cookies" (meaning an electronic link back to another site that is not obvious and often results in spam being sent later to you) or any other Internet paraphernalia attached to the video. One thing you never want to do is send the people reading your newsletter or browsing your website to another site that will in any way harm their computer. There are a lot of sites that will do exactly that. I've found that YouTube.com is a legitimate site and nobody has had any terrible experiences with it that I know about so far, so it seems pretty legitimate and safe - so far.

67.   Reserve an Internet Domain Name That Is <u>Misspelled</u>

While this sounds strange and unusual, it is also one of the smartest and easiest ways to attract unique "hits" on your website. Here's how and why: Many people who use the Internet don't know how various words are spelled. As a result, they often enter the wrong spelling of the website they're trying to find. Since computers don't know when a word is misspelled, they simply take the web surfer to the site they typed in without checking to see if it's the right site for them. In fact, many websites have grown up based upon the misspelling of a word that they've taken advantage of by reserving someone else's misspelled domain name.

If your site can be misspelled, it's a simple thing to reserve every domain name that can be misspelled in any way similar to your website. It is pretty inexpensive to reserve and purchase a domain name on a multi-year basis, so if your domain name can be misspelled, it's a great idea to reserve all possible misspellings. Once you have them, you may simply have the misspelled site "point" prospective visitors to your accurately spelled website. It also stops anyone else from misdirecting potential visitors from your site to their own websites by purposely using the misspelled web address. You'll be surprised at how effective this can be in attracting those visitors who simply make a mistake in spelling your website's name and otherwise would have never contacted you.

68.   Conduct a Survey to Sell a Product or Service

It's a proven fact that people are less resistant to answering a survey than buying something right away on the internet. Take advantage of that simple fact and instead of offering to sell them something directly, ask them to answer a survey before offering them something for free. Only after they've accepted something for free should you go back to sell them anything.

In the holistic practice area this may seem a bit daunting at first, but it's a great way to gain access to potential clients and purchasers of your products. If you make a choice to send out a survey, make it relevant for whoever you send it to and make sure it grabs their interest at the same time. The best way to do both of these things simultaneously is to ask the right questions in your survey. Here's a sample:

Hello,

We're conducting a general survey to see how many people have visited a holistic practitioner during the past three years and what they thought of their effectiveness. Our purpose in asking these questions is to determine how many people believe alternative practitioners are effective in their treatments and how important they are to the general population in their perception. If you'll take a few moments to answer these short and simple questions, we'll gladly give you a FREE download of an extensive article by Theodore W. Robinson outlining ways to overcome financial difficulties during the Recession and explaining how to flourish in the face of hardship.

Here are the questions:

1.   Have you visited an alternative health care provider within the last three (3) years?
        ○ Yes   ○ No

2.   When was the last time you visited an alternative health care professional?
        ○ Less than a month ago   ○ During last six months
        ○ During last year

3.   Did insurance cover the expense of your visits?
        ○ Yes   ○ No   ○ Partially

4.   Did you find the care you received beneficial?
        ○ Yes   ○ No   ○ Partially

5.   Would you use an alternative or complimentary health care professional again?
        ○ Yes   ○ No

6.   Do you believe alternative, complimentary or holistic health care professionals need to be licensed by the state in order to provide you with a margin of safety?
        ○ Yes   ○ No

7.   Would you recommend an alternative health care provider to others?
        ○ Yes   ○ No

8.	Would you recommend others stay away from them unless or until they're licensed?

O Yes   O No

9.	Do you believe that all alternative health care professionals are:

O Competent?   O Incompetent?   O Neither

10.	Do you believe the alternative health care providers you've seen were:

O Too expensive   O Too cheap   O Just about right

Once you've gotten them to answer these ten simple questions, you can then determine many things about them. First, you can see if they have any preliminary prejudices for or against alternative health care practitioners. Second, you can tell if they were willing to pay for such services without the benefit of insurance coverage. Third, you can tell if they were satisfied with the treatment they received. Fourth, you can determine if they would recommend such care to others. Fifth, you can tell whether they thought the cost was too high, low or just right.

Most importantly, however, is the fact that once they've filled out the questionnaire you offer to give them a free download and that's when you get their email address. That increases your email list and confirms that they want to receive your email in the future. Of course, you should always have an auto responder that verifies and confirms that they want to receive your newsletters and email offerings or whatever you send them could be considered Spam under the CANSPAM Act of 2003. However, by doing it this way, you'll find that you're in a trusted position and they're much more likely to accept your future offerings and perhaps buy one of your products or make an appointment to see you for a treatment. Either way, this is a simple soft sell approach that works much more effectively than a straight forward sales approach.

Of course, you should change the survey to support whatever you intend to survey them about so it makes sense within the context of your practice. You may modify or improve any aspect of the sample survey to suit your needs, but always offer them something for free and you'll see a much better response rate from your e-mailings.

69. Link Your Website with Related <u>and</u> Unrelated Websites

By linking your website with other related web sites, you will improve your standings on the various search engines. That means that when someone goes looking for the type of services or products you're offering on your web site, they will type in a few descriptive words into their computer trying to find you or someone like you. If you're one of the first few web sites to be reported by them, there's a much better chance that they'll choose you than someone on a later page. In fact, statistics show that approximately 85% of all viewers click on a website within the first 3-4 listed on the first page of a search engine search. And almost none go beyond the first three pages of the search return unless they're searching for their own name. Therefore, it's vastly important for you to be among the first few web sites mentioned on the search return if you want to be chosen. As mentioned earlier, one way to do this is pay for it by bidding on the metatag words that best describe you and your practice or product. The other way is to simply be first on the list "organically" by having the highest rating. While those ratings vary among search engines, the methods that each one uses rely heavily upon how many links you have to other web sites. It is very important to have as many legitimate links to other web sites if you want to keep your standing as high as possible without having to pay for that privilege.

One way to build your links is to write an email or a letter to webmasters of other sites you admire or would like to link to and ask them to reciprocally link to each other's sites. However, since many webmasters are out there seeking to link with others, many requests get turned down because they don't want just anyone linking to their site. There is another way to accomplish this that works like a charm. Give the other webmasters a telephone call and ask them in person if they would like to reciprocally link both of your web sites together so you both benefit. Most of them will immediately go along with your request once they take a look at your site and verify it's a good looking site and will benefit them and their site if they do so. Mostly, however, they are more willing to link up with you if they speak to you on the phone than by getting an email. It just works better.

70. Post Your Name and Professional Credentials on Websites That Offer Expert Opinions for Legal Trials

This can be a very valuable means of being qualified as a legally sufficient expert and viewed as an expert in your field. Once a Judge of a Court of competent jurisdiction declares you to be an expert in a trial, you are thereafter considered an expert for all time by future Judges. Of course, you must first be recognized and declared an expert by a Judge and before that can happen, you must establish and prove your credentials and experience in the field in which you're about to testify. That means providing the court with testimony and/or evidence of your graduation from various schools of higher education, certifications, licensing and other credentials that would clearly indicate you have the necessary schooling and training to be considered an expert.

Then, you must give testimony as to your specific experience in the field about which you're attempting to establish yourself as an expert. Of course, this type of testimony is subject to cross-examination by the opposing party who is often trying to keep you from being certified as an expert. That can be somewhat challenging, but once it is over and you've been declared an expert who can testify about your field of expertise, it can make a big difference in your overall expert reputation. It also gets added to your *curriculum vitae* and/or biography for future reference and it will usually be relied upon by future Judges if you are called by any party in the future to testify in a law suit. Remember, since Judges ultimately determine most issues of fact within our society, such a distinction goes a long way in many circles and will help you fully establish yourself as an expert in your field.

71.   Join "Second Life" and Offer Classes

Second Life (secondlife.com) is a fairly recent Internet sensation. In Second Life, people join and establish their own Avatar. Their Avatar is effectively their alter ego and they get to design their Avatar in any way they wish. They get to determine the body size, shape, color and hair. They can also dress their Avatar any way they wish. In effect, it can be a way to live a completely different "second life" on the Internet. In fact, you get to interact with other Avatars throughout Second Life in a variety of ways and make contacts. You can also take various classes on Second Life.

If you wish to take a class, all you have to do is arrive at a "Sym" (meaning simulation) and attend a lecture or class that is being given by another Avatar. If you wish to give a class, you must first locate a Sym and be asked by the owner of the Sym to give such a class as a guest speaker. If they approve you, you'll be the Avatar to give your lecture, speech or workshop directly from your own computer in a live setting. You'll actually have the ability to interact with other Avatars who are in your Sym and who may have questions sent to you that may prompt answers from you. As word gets around, the crowds can grow. However, don't expect to attract more than a 10-15 people to one of these lectures. If you attract more than 30 avatars, you're in the mega-star category. Nonetheless, those people who attend could be from anywhere around the world and that means that you're reputation will travel around the world too - in cyberspace - and then to the real people they represent.

72.   Add an Audio Clip on the Opening Page of Your Website

Many websites today have an opening page that includes an audio introduction from the primary person who operates the site. It usually says something welcoming or congratulatory at the outset for finding the site and then may give the visitor a short introduction to where things are located on the site or anything else you may want to include. This is especially helpful if you have a good voice to use or if you have something special you wish to preview for new visitors. You can use almost any type of recording device (including the Edirol mentioned before to your own computer with a microphone attached to it) to first make a recording and then it is only a matter of posting it to your website, which your Webmaster should be easily able to do for you. Of course, it is important to give the viewer the ability to mute the audio if it disturbs them or if it distracts them. Other than that, an audio welcome can make many visitors feel welcomed and comfortable while they're on your web site. It can be a good addition.

73.   Content is King on the Internet

Nothing is more important on the Internet than content! It's what keeps people coming back to your website and reading whatever it is you have to offer. And NEW Content is even more important because the Internet moves along so fast, you must constantly be offering new information or those who have previously visited your website won't come back. That's why once you have a website, it is important to keep filling it with new content all the time. It is also important to use different types of content such as videos, podcasts and references to other sites or information. All of this keeps the minds of those visiting your site active and interested and that's what drives web traffic to your website.

Today's web audience expects to see fresh material all the time and having regularly-updated content will keep them coming back to any site they like and which has regular fresh content. This has been mentioned within the context of article writing, but it is important enough to mention again here. Content is king on the Internet. If you viewers like what you write, they'll want to read more. Once they want to read more, they'll return to your site and your newsletters more regularly. That keeps your name and website in their minds and whenever they need you, they'll remember you. That's as simple as it gets, but is also as important as it gets. Keep creating fresh content and you'll see your website audience grow over time.

74.   Include Interactive Pages onto Your Website

If your present website is just informational in nature, make sure to add discussion boards, comments and responses, questions and anything else that cultivates responses from readers. These type of pages help to build community within those who visit your website. If you send them information or your own comments about whatever is going on in the world, give them an opportunity to respond to you. That way, when someone responds, it may trigger someone else to respond to their comment. That's the way a discussion board gets started and becomes a compelling feature of a website. It can eventually be a place where diverse people can meet and interact with the primary subject being whatever it is your website is all about.

It also gives you an opportunity to interact with your subscribers so you can be heard on a particular topic. Of course, this can take a lot of time and energy and you may eventually feel like you're tied to your computer, but it does establish a central point that many people can interact through on your website and once you get it started, it's hard to stop it. This can be a good thing because every time someone goes to your website to check on their question or comment, it is to your benefit. They're increasing your site's "traffic," which is the number of independent visits it gets from unique visitors and the more the better. Traffic is what determines your standing on the search engines and that determines how high you appear when someone searches for you or your practice.

Bulletin boards are a way for visitors to your site to post messages for other visitors to read. They also work to establish and continue a sense of community and gives visitors yet another reason for going to your site regularly which, again, increases your traffic. Of course, the down side of these offerings is you must have somebody who watches the site regularly so that nobody posts things that could embarrass you on the Internet. There are many irresponsible people out there in cyberspace who love to fool around on other people's web sites and run amok as much as they can and think it's cute or cool. So you must be aware of that type of interference and take measures to control it by having a monitor who watches your site regularly and who has the power to regulate what goes onto it.

By allowing visitors to ask you questions on your site, you are giving them an opportunity to openly ask whatever it is they want to know and it gives you the opportunity to answer them in the same forum - sometimes in real time. By setting up a question and answer forum, you're giving everyone who visits your site an opportunity to learn at the same time as they browse. It also does two other things. It keeps your responses in front of them and all other visitors who go to your site and it increases your site's traffic.

75.   Conduct a Webinar

A webinar is actually a combination of words that describes a specific type of Web conferencing that is used to conduct live meetings or presentations over the Internet. In a webinar, each participant sits at their own computer and is connected to all the other participants in the webinar via the internet. It can be done by either downloading an application on each of the attendees computers or as a web-based application where the students simply enter a URL (website address) to enter the conference. Of course, this has to be set up ahead of time and it will take special programming to accomplish it. You can find this type of programming on the internet by typing in "webinar programming" on any search engine.

A webinar is usually a one-way teaching device from the speaker to the audience in which the audience has limited interaction. However, some webinars allow for interactive question and answer periods as well as polling abilities between the audience and the presenter. Sometimes, the presenter may choose to speak over the computer or over a standard telephone line, which allows him/her to point out specific information being presented on screen simultaneously. In such instances, the audience can then respond over their own telephones lines or by computer email or instant messaging and the presenter can respond to them as part of the webinar. It is usually best to have someone else monitoring these instant messages so you are not distracted while doing the rest of your talk.

There are now web conferencing technologies that allow for the use of VoIP audio technology, which allows for web-based communication like audio over computer. In some situations, webinars also allow for anonymous participant ability, which enables another person to be on line with the rest of the class and most other participants would be unaware of their presence. This can be helpful when you want another expert to provide information to you without anyone else being aware of it.

A webinar can be used for instructing students or updating previous students on new developments in a specific area of practice. It can also be used to stay in contact with longer term students who need supervision over time. This is an inexpensive and effective way to stay in touch with a group of students/affiliates and show them information on their computers simultaneously. You may wish to use webinars within your practice or you may use them with affiliates to keep them up to date on new products and developments in your practice. You can also use this in a similar fashion to teleseminars, only with a webinar, you get the added advantage of having a computer screen with which you can display color slides, moving pictures or any number of other alternatives. Use your own imagination to determine whether webinars are for you and your practice.

76. Form Partnerships with Other who have Email Lists to Promote Each Other's Emails and Web Sites

By forming partnerships with other email owners both you and the other owner are benefitting each other simultaneously. Of course, there are a few prerequisites to consider before making a commitment to another owner. First, never give them direct access to your email list. If you do let them see and use your list, they may use it in a fashion that could deteriorate it by overuse or some other means and render it useless to you afterward. Remember, you worked hard to establish your readership, don't give it away easily.

Second, make sure that their email list is well qualified. That means that the people who they have on their list actually are people of standing who want to receive their newsletter and won't simply reject it as soon as it comes in.

Next, make sure that you both have about the same number of recipients on your email lists before you casually promote another person's site. If they have fewer names than you, then perhaps there's a way for you to get some other compensation for sharing your list with them. Make sure that if you're promoting someone else's email or website that they have a different type of crowd than you do who receives their email. That way, there is no direct competition between you and them.

Once you have all that out of the way, then it's a great idea to tell your email list about someone else's email and/or website if you think they're great and you would like to recommend them to others. This is especially so if they're going to recommend your email and web site to their readership simultaneously.

Another thing to remember is that you should both agree to retain some editorial oversight and approval of how the other site is going to present you and your site to their readers. Of course, you should offer the same opportunity to the other site owner to oversee your written offerings just as you should be able to review his/hers before it goes out to their readers. Use this opportunity sparingly since nobody wants anyone looking over the shoulder constantly, but its still a good idea to retain the ability to do so.

77.   Submit Comments on Other Authors Books on Any Website That Carries Books

Amazon.com is an international website that sells all types of consumer items, most notably books from all over the world. As part of their website, they display many books and give all the details about them on their site. They also invite comments and grading from readers about each book. One way to gain additional notice and notoriety (albeit limited at best) is to offer your own comments on other authors' books. Of course, only do so if you've read the entire book and only make legitimate comments. But if you've read it and liked it, then be certain to offer your own comment. At the end of the comment, you can usually also add whatever additional professional information you wish and that's where you can add your professional credentials and any other pertinent information. You'd be surprised at how just about every author looks at the comments underneath his/her own book and if they notice your name and information after a particularly well crafted positive comment, it's likely that when you go to publish your own book, you may be able to ask them for a reciprocal comment on Amazon or elsewhere, including the back cover of your book.

78.   Change the Metatags on Your Website

Metatags are descriptive words attached to each web page of your website that are like little titles or definitions for the search engines to find and discover whatever they're looking for. If the metatags reflect everything that's on a particular page, the search engine will verify that fact and make a positive finding that the title and content are consistent. This is important because if they're not consistent, it will actually work against you. It is important to make certain that those tag words are also included within the title or at least in the first few paragraphs of each page they're on. This is where the search engines primarily search to verify consistency. If they're not in the first few paragraphs, rewrite your page and make sure they show up there in the future. It will make a big difference to you standing in the search engines and that is important.

Remember, it is very important to show up on the first page of any search result and it is even more important to show up in the first three spots of any first search page. Most people searching the web are impatient and usually they won't look further than the first three pages at most - and that's if they're doing a hard core search. Otherwise, the vast majority of people searching for just about anything on the Internet only go to the first three to six returns on any search. However, since each search engine goes about determining how to prioritize who hits the top three and beyond, it changes between engines all the time. What you want to do is make certain that your site shows up in that top three organically or through pay-per-click advertisements.

79. Use Search Engine Optimization Techniques to Get a Higher Natural Search Engine Listing

Website optimization is a very powerful means of increasing your traffic to your website. It takes a number of different means to increase traffic, but when you do, it can make a big difference in your search engine standing. Search engine standings means where you come up on a search when a descriptive word or words are typed into Google, Yahoo or any other search engine describing you.

It has been estimated that there are over 5 billion web pages on the Internet today and it is growing every day. Studies have proven that about 85% of all searches are ended before the viewer reaches the end of the first page and most of the time it ends before they hit the fifth or sixth entry. So it is vastly important to be among the top few results on any pertinent word search. The search engines all use different criteria for how they report their results. Most use what are known as "spiders" that crawl every website on the web to see what criteria has been met and what the results are for your website. If you want to be found on the first page it takes a considerable amount of work.

Perhaps the most important aspect is to have new and ever-changing content. The search engines watch to see how often your website is updated and upgraded. They also want to see that each web page (which means each distinct page with a different topic on it) is consistent and has meaningful content on it. Another thing they look for is that the metatags which are hidden descriptions of the content that help the search engines find a particular page are consistent with the content on that page. For example, you want to have your metatags reflect what's on that particular page, so if your page is about Emotional Freedom Technique (EFT) then the best metatags would include "Emotional Freedom Technique" and "EFT" as well as "emotional release", "stress reduction", "acupressure", "therapy", "therapeutic", etc. You can see how these words all relate to what EFT does for people and that would also be explained within the web page itself.

Other ways to optimize one's website are to simply have all your friends and family click on your website as often as possible. That's because one of the parameters for being high in the rankings is the number of unique visitors who actually click on your website. The higher the number, the better your standings. You can also put a click connection from any newsletter article you've written and have it connect directly to your website. That way, when readers get down to a certain part of your article and want to read the rest of it, they have to click on to your website to finish it. That brings more traffic to your website and increases your standings again.

80. Submit Your Articles or Book Excerpts to Other Web Sites with Links Back to Your Website

When you've written your own articles for your website, you may find there are others that just don't fit your site. Rather than discard them, you can offer them to other non-competing web sites so they can publish them. Some will simply pay you for your articles and some will accept a barter or reciprocal arrangement that allows you to link both web sites together and offer each other's articles to the other site. By doing this both sites get to display new articles and offer something different to their readers. It also costs less money to do it this way and the best part is that both sites get more traffic than they would otherwise because each is linking to the other. The same holds true for using excerpts from a book you may have written. Once you finish writing it, make sure to offer various excerpts to other sites so they will have more new content and you'll have an additional outlet for viewers to read it and hence build an interest in buying your book.

81. Build Profiles on Popular Social Networking Sites Such as Myspace, Facebook, or Linkedin

When you build a profile on any of the popular social networking sites, you can then use your profiles to connect to other people with similar interests to your own and you can direct them to your web site at some point along the way. This may sound like "kids stuff" but it is turning into a very popular way of keeping in touch with people of all ages and it helps to meet people on the Internet. As you meet new people, you'll find that there will come a time when they want to learn more about you and that's when you can direct them to your web site. Or, you may wish to add their email address to your newsletter list and stay in touch with them that way. Either way, it's a great way to not only stay in touch, but to establish an entirely new group of acquaintances and potential people who may wish to attend your workshops, seminars and call for private sessions once they discover exactly what you do.

While this may sound questionable to most professionals, remember, a number of celebrities have already put their personal and professional information on Facebook.com and are watching to see what responses they get to it. More importantly, the Internet is populated by younger people who have money with which to do things and they use Facebook and other similar sites to meet and connect with other people and professionals alike. If you want to access that segment of society, seriously consider posting your information on networking sites and monitor the responses you get.

Similar to posting on Facebook.com strongly consider going onto Yahoo.com and join one of their social groups. You may also join Linkedin.com or any number of other social or business contact groups. Start by entering your personal information and professional information and friends and/or business associates and see what type of responses you get from them. A huge segment of our population is now frequenting these types of sites and connecting with each other for personal reasons and it is likely to expand in the future. While joining this type of group used to appear to be less than professional, it is now starting to become acceptable and the more businesspeople who use these type of sites, the more acceptable it will become.

82.   Start Social Bookmarking

Social Bookmarking is a way to bring people together via computers effectively and easily. One site you can use is Del.icio.us which is a centralized site for starting to be part of a social network. The reason you may wish to do this is because it allows you to interact with others in your social group and see what web sites others in your group are viewing. That way everyone can benefit from any new sites anyone in the group has happened upon. It is also a reciprocal arrangement, so everyone can benefit from whatever anyone else has found as well.

To get started, go to Del.icio.us and start at the registration page to establish a free account. When you get on the page, you will be asked to enter some personal information which will include your user name and a password to enter the site. At the same time it will give you the opportunity to add two buttons that are important to add.

They are the "tag" button which is how you'll add new bookmarks to the website and the Del.icio.us button which allows you to access the site. The "tag" button allows you to simply click on that button whenever you like a particular website and it will automatically be added to your section of the site.

At the same time you click on the tag button, a box will automatically open up and give you the opportunity to register a "tag" word or words for that site. That way, if everyone in your group is looking for the same type of websites, all you do is use the same tag for all of them and every one of them that's been discovered by anyone in the group will be automatically organized for your later use.

The tag words are important since as you add more tag words on to any particular site you register with, the more access words you have to get back to it again. It also gives you the ability to organize all of the various sites you've tagged by specific words and then put all of one type in the same category. Then, when you want to go back to that category, just type in that tag word and it will deliver all of the sites with that word as part of its tag words.

The reason its called a "social network" is because the tags on Del.icio.us are public. Anyone can access them. If you've accumulated a lot of pertinent sites on a particular topic and they have all been categorized with the same tag word, they are accessible to anyone else who looks up that word. This allows others to get the benefit of your research and you get the benefit of knowing you're sharing your knowledge and/or research. But, even more importantly, you get the benefit of access to their bookmarking just like they can access yours. In other words it works both ways.

In order to use this technique in marketing, one approach is to do your own research and add tagged sites to De.licio.us and then allow others to do the same. However, in your case, you have the option of adding your own website to De.licio.us and any other websites that are similar or related and add your own tags that include descriptive words that describe your own site. Anyone looking for any of your tag words will automatically access your website and bring more traffic to it and again, that means higher standings on the search engines.

For more information on this topic, you can go to YouTube and search for videos on social bookmarking.

TARGETED SEMINARS AND WORKSHOPS

This section was added because a lot of practitioners overlook the prospect of targeting specific workshops to attract specific audiences. By targeting different types of attendees, you can present yourself as "The Expert" in a particular field that may, in fact, be one of many you practice. By targeting only one group, you can present yourself as the apparent expert in that area alone. This is because most people's experience is that an expert can only be expert in one area of practice and even if that's not entirely true, they'll usually shy away from anyone who tries to present themselves as expert at more than one thing at a time. So just stay with one area initially and then, after you've impressed them with your expertise in that field, you can expose them to other areas in which you also excel. Here are a number of ideas and concepts for offering specific workshops and seminars that will open the door to new areas of concentration.

83.   Conduct Teleseminars

Telephone seminars (teleseminars) are one of the latest and best ways to hold a seminar without having the students travel to a particular location. With astronomically high gasoline prices and low cost telephone services, this is the ideal way to conduct classes.

There are many ways to approach these type of classes. One of the easiest is to establish a conference call number and announce in an email to your email list and on your website that everyone can listen in for free. In fact, you should tell them to invite their friends to listen for free as well.

Of course, to access the teleseminar, they'll have to first obtain a contact number or access code which they will only be able to get by entering their email address. That way, you can collect additional email addresses for your list. Once you've given them an access code, they can then dial up the teleseminar number and listen in to your seminar for free and you've come away with their email address for future use.

In this type of seminar, you give them enough information in the seminar to make it interesting and informative, but not so much that they can do it themselves without obtaining further information from you. That way, you can use the free teleseminar as a draw for them to attend paid teleseminars or to purchase CD or DVD collections from you with the in-depth information included in it.

There are many variations on this theme, but they are all intended to allow people from remote locations to take part in a short workshop or lecture of an hour or more at a much reduced cost. This is an ideal way to conduct training for people all over the country or world at limited expense to them and you can keep your connection with them simultaneously.

Another way to conduct such teleseminars is to have a class in which a number of people physically attend and are allowed to ask questions and make comments during the talk or at the end. Those that call in can also ask questions verbally through an intermediary or may be relegated to writing in through email or IMs (Instant Messages). You can have an assistant monitoring those communications and tell you which you might want to answer or to delete the ones that don't apply to the topic or are too long. This is one of the means by which lecturers on SecondLife.com conduct their lectures and the lecturers will often respond immediately to the emails they receive.

Again, there are many variations, but the optimum way to conduct these teleseminars is to have the callers pay a subscription fee annually or on a per session basis so they have a vested interest in attending. Sometimes the annual fee can be tied into joining as a member of a particular group and the teleseminars are part of the benefits of membership. Other times they can simply be a package pricing for five or ten sessions at a reduced rate.

As you're setting up your teleseminar, it's a good idea to have it recorded so you can offer it in its entirety later as an MP3 download, a CD or a Podcast. Some telephone systems will do this for you, but they charge you for it afterward. Otherwise, its best to record it on your own equipment. You can charge for all of these extra products and that's another way to pay for your time and efforts in conducting the teleseminar in the first place.

To establish a conference call phone number you must first decide which system you wish to use. There are a number of conference calling services listed that all have pretty consistent pricing. I suggest you type in "teleconferencing" on any search engine and you'll find a bunch of them. They are all pretty much alike, but their services and prices will vary amongst them. Make your own choice.

Here are a few practical tips you will want to follow to make sure your teleseminar is successful:

a.   First, decide what topic you wish to talk about. If you can't think of something you feel would draw listeners or you don't think you have enough knowledge to talk about something for an hour, then ask someone who you consider to be an expert if you can interview them. All experts love to be interviewed so they can show off what they know and it helps them market themselves and their products. In the meanwhile, it gives you experience and starts the ball rolling.

b.   Make sure you know how to use your phone conferencing service before you start. Otherwise, you could get started and not know what to do or how to use it once you have people on the line with you. That could be embarrassing. You can find these services on any search engine by typing in "teleseminars" or "teleconferences."

c.   Learn how to read and respond to email questions or comments that come in while you're giving your seminar.

d.   Prepare an outline of what you're going to speak about and make sure you follow it. You'll look far more professional doing it this way, rather than doing it extemporaneously. Proper prior planning also eliminates the prospect of thinking nobody is going to call in and then, once you're on the phone more people call in than you expected and you find yourself unprepared. It is always better to be prepared and nobody shows up than being unprepared and everybody shows up.

e.   Since you are giving an audio seminar, make sure you go over new things slowly or repeatedly. Remember, when people are listening, they only retain about 15% of what they hear, so it's best to give them more than one opportunity to learn from you.

f.   Since many people who wanted to be on your teleseminar may miss it, make sure you either repeat it again a few hours or days later or make it available as a podcast to them for a small fee. Many teleconference phone companies provide this service as part of their overall services and some charge additionally for it. If you record your teleseminar yourself, you can then download it into a CD or MP-3 and sell it independently later or put it into an accessible archive for anyone to listen to through your website.

g.   Make sure your telephone equipment is working properly and not sending out any static or have any other problems. There's nothing worse than doing all your advertising and getting everyone on the line with you and they don't stay because your telephone equipment is interfering with the call. Check it and recheck it beforehand.

h.   Plan ahead. If you're going to sell a product of any sort during your teleseminar, make sure you have all your information prepared and the price set in stone well ahead of time. If you really want to market something, make sure you have all your marketing concepts down pat long before you send out the first email telling everyone about it. That way, you're prepared and if anyone has a question, you'll have a ready answer available to answer them. You'll also look a lot more professional by being prepared.

      i.   Even if nobody shows up for your teleseminar, do it anyway. First, you'll get some experience by doing it. Second, make sure you record it and then offer it later on your archive, CD, MP-3 or podcast. Don't get thrown if nobody shows up. View it as an opportunity to hone your speaking skills so the next time you'll be even better.

All of these ideas and suggestions will eventually be helpful to you in establishing yourself in your field as an expert of national or perhaps international standing. Doing teleseminars can lead the way to that distinction and the resultant following it attracts. They also serve to build traffic to your website and your overall business and build a product line for you with the passage of time as you do more of them.

84.   Conduct Specific Seminars about Different Issues You Treat

Formulate a seminar/workshop around each specific area in which you work. That way, you will not only draw attention to your own expertise in that particular area, you will attract people who are interested in it to your office. This will further establish you as an expert in the field and get you more referrals from those that attend as well as those who don't attend, but who received your invitation and noted it in their mind or heard about it later and were impressed with the topic and the fact that you were teaching it.

Whenever you hold such an event, it is important to build it up with press releases, advertisements, emails, newsletters, mailings and anything else you can think of to bring attention to the fact that you're running a workshop or seminar. That way, even if someone can't make it to the event, they'll know you're running it and recognize you have sufficient expertise in the field to teach it to others. That's a benefit in and of itself since that's how you build your reputation within the community and within the professional community as well.

Remember, during the last five to ten minutes, after you've completed your teaching and questions and answer period, get evaluation sheets filled out by everyone who attended. It not only provides the students a means of giving you feedback, it will give you insights into your teaching abilities and how they can be improved. It also automatically provides you with testimonials that can be used later in your advertising. Here's a sample:

STUDENT EVALUATION FORM

Your Name _____ Date of Class:_____

Instructor's name_____

Class Level attended?

_____ EFT Level 1 Basic

_____ EFT Level 2 Intermediate

_____ EFT Level 3 Ultimate Therapist

_____ Smoking Cessation

_____ IET Level _____

_____ Other (Name of Course)_____

We value your opinion. Please inform us of how we can make this workshop better for others in the future.

Please circle your evaluation of the following questions. Your feedback helps us determine what we can do better; what we're doing well and how we can keep our programs fresh, informative and useful to our students. By signing below you agree we can use your testimonial in the future in our advertising. We trust that's okay with you as we want others to know what our students thought of our classes. If not, check here. ____

Was the information presented so that you understood it?

1   2   3   4   5   6   7   8   9   10

Did you feel like you were able to ask questions easily?

1   2   3   4   5   6   7   8   9   10

Was the teacher knowledgeable about the subject?

1   2   3   4 5   6   7   8   9   10

Did the teacher honor your needs throughout the instruction?

1   2   3   4 5   6   7   8   9   10

Was the price of the class too little, about right, or too high?

_____

Was the length of the training sufficient to learn everything you wanted?

_____

Was there enough hands on training/practice to satisfy your needs?

1   2   3   4 5   6   7   8   9   10

How did you find out about us and this program?

_____

Would you like to be informed of other interesting programs in the future?

_____

Please offer any additional comments. Thanks for your help.

_____

_____

_____

_____

Sign here _____

Make sure to include a number of lines for comments and encourage testimonials from the attendees. This can be very important because when they've just finished learning something compelling and they're enthusiastic, they're more likely to give you a glowing testimonial which you can later use to promote your class again. Testimonials are the "Mothers Milk" of advertisements because people who have already attended have said you did a great job and that helps relieve the anxiety from those considering future workshops. If they find some fault with the job you did, use it to correct or improve your future workshops. These evaluation sheets can be a very important asset to you and your practice if you review them and pay attention to them.

Notice on the sample form that we've included a waiver of usage built into the evaluation sheet so you'll have their permission to use their testimonial without seeking it later and when they may not be able to be reached.

Of course, you can change this form in any fashion you see fit to make it work best for your needs, however, remember to always include the waiver in the body of the wording so you'll be able to use their comments as testimonials in the future.

85.   Conduct Low Cost Group Therapy Sessions

If your particular modality applies to this (such as EFT, Hypnosis, etc.) you may wish to offer to conduct low cost group therapy sessions. They are a great way to share your talents with a larger group of people and with those who might not otherwise be able to afford your individualized services. It also gives many people the opportunity to experience what you do for a lower introductory fee and gives them the option of watching you work within a group so they can evaluate whether they want to seek you out for a private session for more personal issues.

Group sessions are interesting and insightful and can make you more money than you initially expect, since as more people attend, even at a low entry cost, you will still earn a substantial income for each session. Remember, if you can work with one client at a time, you can usually work with ten or more at a time without much extra effort. That's because the group wants to work together and will usually accept you as their leader and foster that leadership as the group progresses.

Groups are especially interesting because they offer a unique environment in which people can see others heal themselves in their presence and that usually gives them the courage and insights that allows them to do it too. Group therapy can be especially compelling for many people because they see it work on others and then they feel less hopeless about their own condition. Groups can sometimes be difficult to control, but if you're careful and take full control of whatever goes on in the group, you'll soon find that they'll look to you for leadership and will want to follow your lead, especially if it means that they might be able to heal whatever is upsetting or painful to them.

The energy of working with a number of people at once also gives the entire group a different feeling than during a private session. Many times a person may not know where to start with a particular issue and by sitting in a group, they get the chance to hear others speak and work on similar issues and it breaks them loose to do whatever they need to do to heal. Often times in a group environment, people will also see that they're not alone in their suffering about a similar problem and they realize that something can be done about it, when, up until that moment, they felt helpless and alone. This is a very hopeful situation and works well for many people. It also works well for the therapist because it offers an introduction into their field of endeavor and helps them feel more comfortable within a group setting. Group therapy can be a very enjoyable aspect of your practice.

86. Offer Special Programs Tailored to Specific Groups or Issues

a. Offer Public Speaking Anxiety Reduction Workshops

Fear of public speaking is the number one fear in society. That's right, people worry about public speaking more than they worry about death. In fact, fear of public speaking transcends every walk of life and every position in life. Yet, most people have no idea of how to eliminate this fear other than through relaxation drugs that then make you drowsy and that doesn't work too well when you have to speak to a thousand people at a convention.

If you have an EFT or Hypnosis type of practice, you already know you have the answer to those people's prayers who suffer from this type of fear. In fact, this is one of the types of services that if you can guarantee success, you can charge by the outcome. Remember, CEOs and high powered executives and governmental officials all have to speak to crowds of people who are constantly judging them and to whom they are answerable. That leads to a huge amount of anxiety and stress for most public speakers. If you can eliminate those fears, you have a very valuable ability for which you may demand just compensation.

This is a very powerful class, workshop, seminar or retreat to conduct and once you start to be successful with your students, the word will get out and you'll be inundated with new students.

b.   Do Stress Reduction Courses for Test Taking Anxiety

As most people know, taking any kind of test can be highly stressful, but taking a Scholastic Aptitude Test (SAT) or a Law School Admission Test (LSAT) or any of the Medical or Dental Boards are extremely stressful because they play a large role in determining whether you get into a school of higher learning or not. In effect, everything is riding on that one test, so the stress runs very high.

If you have the type of alternative practice that can help reduce that stress, then you have something very valuable to most of those test takers. Practitioners of Hypnosis, Emotional Freedom Technique and a host of other modalities have the capacity to help those students relieve their stress completely and allow them to take their test with a cooler head and without stress. This is a valuable ability and if it is offered to SAT or LSAT preparation teachers, it could improve their percentages of students improving their scores, which increases their ability to sign more students up for their courses in the future. It would also lead to a lucrative business for you.

There are many different types of preparation courses and they vary in different parts of the country. You can locate them in your local telephone directory or on the Internet by typing in "SAT preparation courses" or the like in any search engine and you'll get immediate results. Once you get their name and email address, contact them and speak with whoever runs the course. Offer to improve their students scores by at least 10 points and see what they say. If they agree to hire you, offer to do whatever work you do for a certain base fee and then a percentage of any increase in their business each time they do another course. This adjunct to their course will not only help students get higher scores (provided you can accomplish the task), it will also give you a great reputation among those very students after they're in schools of higher education and beyond which means they may contact you again long after they've graduated and are in the business world. Stress reduction is one of the most valuable talents any practitioner can share with the world.

c.   Offer Special Programs for Children

Offering a special program for children is an excellent way for that segment of each family in your practice to become engaged with and helped by you. As a general rule, parents will do almost anything for their children and if you can provide a valuable service to them, you'll have them in your office regularly. When the parents see improvements in their children, they'll want some too. The real question is what can you specifically offer to help children within the realm of your office practice? One thing we've noticed is that children learn best from other children. So if you have anything within your practice that fits the bill, then find a young teenager, teach him or her the ropes of what you want taught to other children about what it is you do and schedule some workshops for kids. Of course, always have adult supervision at all times, but let the kids teach each other. They'll learn better and the kids who teach will gain a great deal of self-confidence and will actually learn it better because they have to re-order it in their brains in order to teach it and that's the best way to learn.

There are other benefits to this type of arrangement as well. It builds a sense of community within your practice because kids tend to talk to other kids and if they like what they learn, they'll tell other kids and that will in turn draw more kids to sign up. Of course, you have to have this set up in advance, so if you want to sell them other products, you'll have to have any products or workshops available ahead of time. While it takes some planning and work beforehand, it can be a very worthwhile endeavor for your practice and will increase your practice's sense of community and build your practice.

d.   Offer Unique Programs for Couples

If you work with couples in your practice, let the public know about it by offering special programs just for couples. Workshops/seminars specifically directed at couples and the problems that come with being a couple are very useful and helpful and bring big benefits to your clients as well as your practice. Couples work is not easy, but it is very rewarding when you see a couple in trouble pull themselves back from the brink of disaster with your help. It also bears witness to your expertise and abilities in this field and this again leads to referrals of other couples as well as individuals in the future.

When offering couples programs, its important to remember that you want to appeal to both parties regardless of your own predilections. In couples work, either party can be having a problem and it may go deeper than it originally appears. Watch for clues to see what it is that you want to address with each couple, but only do couples work if you have the necessary education and experience.

If you are teaching a workshop/seminar with couples, make sure that you have someone from each gender in attendance so that neither side of the couple feels like they're being put upon because they find themselves in a gender minority.

Once you've helped a couple resolve what's been coming between them, make sure you get a testimonial from them so you can add it to your brochure, article or pamphlet later on couple's issues.

e.   Offer to reduce Stress for a Human Resources Staff

What could be better than offering a stress reduction class or workshop to human resource employees who have to deal with every type of problem possible. HR staff deal with everything from pregnancy to drugs and all those problems with staff that funnel through that office. They're under a huge amount of stress on a daily basis. They're also charged by management with being humane to employees and treating them with dignity and decency - even when they'd prefer to do otherwise. That puts even more stress on them. Human resource employees are almost always under a great deal of stress and they usually can't leave their office for any length of time because something is always coming up that needs their attention. That's where you come it.

If you offer to run a workshop right in their office to reduce their stress and you're successful at it, you'll have an instant referral agency at your fingertips. It has been my experience that when someone gets relief, they want to share it with others. Before long, you'll have referrals coming your way from their office and you'll have formed an entirely new stream of income from that one workshop. If you need or want more clients, offer it to another corporation and use the testimonials that you solicit from the first office to get your foot in the door of the next corporation. This can turn into an entire corporate branch of your practice before long.

f.   Offer to Run a Smoking Cessation Workshop at Corporate Headquarters

Most corporations are fully aware of the adverse effects smoking has on their employees. They know it takes a great deal of time away from the job for smoking breaks and it costs them untold amounts of money for medical leave and care when smokers eventually become ill from smoking. Corporations are very interested in helping their employees stop smoking. In fact, they are so motivated that they will gladly offer to allow their employees to leave their posts for awhile to attend a smoking cessation workshop, especially if it is held right in their building.

All that's needed is for you to offer a Stop Smoking program to them and offer to conduct it right on their premises so it can take less time away from their employees jobs. To make an offer, you should first have a complete program prepared in advance setting forth the techniques you use and informing them of your previous experiences and successes. This is where those all-important testimonials come in. You should also show them how much money your program is eventually going to save them and then show them how much any investment of time and/or money that they make will eventually turn into a profit for their company by saving them lost money over time.

It is also important to show them how you're going to be able to motivate their employees to enroll in your workshop and what it will cost them or the employer to join. Many employers are not willing to pay the full cost of such a program, but may be willing to pay a partial payment if their employees are willing to pay the balance themselves. Most employers think they're doing a lot by giving their employees time off to attend during working hours, but the intelligent ones realize the long term benefits of having non-smokers as employees. Remember, every smoker takes a "smoke break" every hour or so during work. That means they leave their job for five to ten minutes four to six times a day. That's about an hour a day lost to smoking. If your seminar takes two hours it is no more than two days of lost time due to smoking.

g.   Offer Your Services to Athletic Teams

This can be a very useful means of developing your skills as well as your practice. If you believe you have the right stuff, talent and expertise to offer your services to a local athletic team, then by all means do so. Many teams have discovered alternative health care works for them when all other strategies and main stream techniques have failed. As a result, they are often willing and interested in using an alternative health care worker, energy worker or some other skilled individual who can do what their team needs in a pinch. Sometimes it's a sore shoulder or a pinched nerve in the back. Sometimes a player or team has lost their will to win. But when a team is desperate to win at all costs, they will turn to just about any alternative method and give it a try. That's when your offering could make a world of difference to them and you alike. This applies to high school sports all the way up to professional teams.

Some alternative healers approach individual coaches and others approach individual athletes in the hope that once they display their expertise on them, they will get referred by the player to the team coaches. If a player recovers quicker than normally expected, the coach will usually be the first to notice and ask if he or she did anything unusual to accomplish such a feat.

Another approach is to find a high school coach and impress him or her by helping their athletes. Then, once the coach sees how well you did for his players, there's a likelihood he/she will tell the professional athletes living in the area about your abilities. Of course, that's a more circuitous route than just going straight to a professional club itself, but it can be difficult to get into a professional setting without having the right credentials. Making connections with high school or college coaches can eventually make a difference as they move up to work in professional sports and bring all their contacts with them. In any event, whatever it takes to get close enough to a professional athlete or team is the right approach and once you've successfully accomplished that and prove what you can do for them, you'll more than likely become a regular fixture around the clubhouse after that.

h.   Offer a Stress Reduction Workshop for Teachers

School teachers are about the most stressed out people in our society. Just imagine having to cope with your children all day long, while you try to teach them things they have little or no interest in and then try to get them to get good grades. Now multiply it by 25-30 children at once. That's stress with a capital S. One way to spread the word about what you do and give back to the community at the same time is to offer complimentary stress reduction workshops (if they apply to the specific type of alternative work you do) to the teachers in your community or a specific school.

The workshops can be offered during school vacations, summer break or on weekends depending upon your needs as well as the needs of the teachers. Whatever you decide to offer, make sure it is well done and that the teachers actually experience a reduction in their stress levels. When you accomplish that, you'll quickly gain an excellent reputation among a very closely tied group of professionals and they talk amongst themselves as well as with their parents and students. It's a great way to get your reputation established in short order, increase your practice exponentially and give back to the community simultaneously.

i.   Offer a Complimentary Session to a Politician's Staff

Who is better to offer complimentary services to than a politician? They have more contacts than anyone else in town, they know everyone and everyone knows them. If you impress them, the rest of your town is bound to hear about it. Once they're sufficiently impressed, they will tell family members and their political club and constituents.   Before long, you'll find your telephone ringing by those wanting to experience the relief you've offered to their friend and leader.

Again, word of mouth is incalculable in its power.   Politicians are always speaking to somebody and, like everybody, they love anything that is free.   And then love to tell everybody about it.   But they usually recognize talent when they directly experience it.   If you're talented at what you do, this could be a very good place to start displaying your expertise.   This is especially so when it comes to smoking cessation because almost all municipalities have stop smoking programs in effect and they are all in favor of their employees quitting smoking.   It's a very lucrative area if you work with this specific area and can offer real results.   The same holds true for stress reduction.   If you can actually offer something that will help politicians and their staff relax and de-stress, you will gain a huge advantage and free publicity in the future.   Whatever other benefits you can bestow upon a politician could ultimately become a benefit for you and your practice if they like what you do.   Offer it.   The worst they can do is say no, but most times they'll say yes and that's the beginning.

j.   Offer Stress Reduction Courses for Those Who Audition or Have Stage Fright

Professional performers make acting look effortless, but for those who are trying to find their way into the acting profession, it can be very stressful. In fact, stage fright is quite common among young or inexperienced actors of both genders. (Many experienced actors also have stage fright, but they don't tell anybody and instead cover it up.)   Many an actor has lost an audition because stage fright has made them stiff in front of an audience and only after years of therapy and many blown auditions do they finally bring their fright under some control, but the fear of it arising again always lurks in the back of their mind.

If you and your practice can help eliminate such stress (such as hypnosis, EFT, etc.) then you have a place in the acting field. All you need to do is advertise in the entertainment magazines and newspapers or go on line and list your talents on websites that list acting jobs, interviews and auditions. That's where the actors will be looking for work and that's where you advertisement should be located as well. Always place your advertisements where those you want to contact are going to be looking themselves.

When you advertise this type of technique, its important that you don't overstate your ability to eliminate stage fright. Only make claims which you are absolutely sure you can substantiate through your efforts. However, if you can ultimately eliminate stage fright, then don't hesitate to offer a money back guarantee and that will eliminate any natural skepticism from those who have suffered the longest from stage fright. Once you're eliminated stage fright from a few actors, their friends will discover you and eventually producers, directors and studios will be calling your number and asking for help for one or more of their actors. It's an invaluable talent and you should make certain to be adequately paid for your success in this field.

k.   Offer Stress Reduction Courses for Professionals

Stress is a major factor in most people's lives, but it is especially important in professionals' lives and especially among surgeons, trial lawyers and public speakers. Those are people who hold people's lives literally in their hands and must perform flawlessly or they're held liable to legal sanctions. They are under a lot of pressure and stress just by virtue of their jobs. I can personally tell you as a young trial lawyer that every time I started a trial, my knees would actually shake and I'd often "get sick" the day of trial. Of course, in retrospect, it was all psychosomatic, but at the time, all I knew was I was "too sick" to start that trial. I only caught on to it when I noticed I always seemed to get too sick to appear in court on the starting day of trial at every trial I did for the first few years of my practice.

Had I had any one of the techniques I use now, such as Emotional Freedom Technique or self-hypnosis, not only would I would have not experienced that level of stress, I would have been cool and collected each time I went to trial. The same thing happens to surgeons, dentists, negotiators and every other type of professional who have stressful situations arise in their life.

If your area of expertise is to reduce stress in any fashion, then you have a built in audience of professionals who are motivated clients. All you have to do is inform them of your ability to help them reduce their stress levels and you'll have a packed house every time you run a workshop or seminar on stress reduction.

To inform them, find their Associations and contact the Executive Director of the one you want to speak at, or if they have a speakers Bureau, speak to whoever runs it. Inform them of your talents in this area and suggest a speaking engagement for their members. It is important to be prepared in advance of approaching them. Make sure you have your curriculum vitae with you and a fully prepared program in written form so you can leave it with them or send it to them immediately. That way, they will recognize you're a professional and they will be assured that you'll do an excellent job if they choose to use you for such a speech. Remember, they have to come off as competent to their bosses too, so when you do your speech, they want to look good at the end of it for inviting you in the first place.

When you speak to professionals, look the part yourself. Dress the part of a professional whenever you're speaking to them. Wear a suit or more formal looking attire and go the extra mile to look great. Have professionally prepared hand-outs for distribution and, most importantly, make sure your entire presentation leaves them feeling less stressed. That's the bottom line if you're giving a speech on reducing stress. Make sure they have an experience of leaving with less stress than they came in the door with and you'll be considered a success.

Once you're finished your speech, make yourself available to those who attend to speak with you so they can ask questions or make an appointment to work with you privately. Also, make sure to bring something that you can give away or run a raffle for your book so you get their email addresses when you leave. Professionals are people too and they get nervous and stressed, so if you can do something to help them relieve that stress, you'll find yourself in great demand.

1. **Offer Workshops on Performance Anxiety, Sexually Related Issues or Erectile Dysfunction**

If your particular practice addresses sexual problems or performance issues such as erectile dysfunction, then this is a great area to do workshops in and offer to the general public.

Obviously, erectile dysfunction is a considerable problem within our society or it wouldn't show up all the time on television commercials. If erectile dysfunction is a problem, then you know there are other related sexual problems throughout society that very few people are addressing.

If you're qualified, offer workshops, seminars, lectures and private sessions on sexually related topics as they relate to your type of healing practice. While this can sometimes be a delicate area for many people to discuss in public, if you have the ability to easily speak in public about sexual issues, you'll find there will be a lot of people who will show up to listen and participate if it looks like a professionally presented seminar or workshop.

Most people who suffer from one sexual issue or another feel that they're the only one having that problem and so, most of the time, they don't discuss it with anyone because they're embarrassed or humiliated due to their early upbringing or religious training. There is a huge amount of disinformation and an even larger number of uninformed people who know little to nothing about sex and don't want to bring the subject up or discuss it with anyone because of their fears and embarrassment.

That's where you can offer lectures, seminars and workshops to those who need it the most. If you are able to impart some worthwhile information to those that need it most, you'll have a built in audience and client list after just a few of those type of events. Of course, if you have not training in this area, take the necessary courses first to learn about it and become certified or licensed if that is necessary in your state. Once certified, if you have a natural propensity to work in this area, the world needs you.

m.   Offer Self-Esteem or Self-Confidence Improvement Courses

Many people suffer from low self-esteem and/or have no self-confidence. If your type of practice lends itself to helping others build their self-esteem and self-confidence, you'll have them beating a path to your door in short order once the word gets out that you can help. Of course, it is up to you to start the ball rolling when it comes to getting the word out, but that's been discussed in other areas of this book already.

What's important for you to do is see if your training lends itself to helping others eliminate self-esteem issues and building self-confidence. If it does, then it's time to do as much as you can to start advertising that fact.

The first thing to do is draft a program that works for building self-esteem and self-confidence. To do this, determine what you can do using your modalities to accomplish such a goal. Then set up your program and plan it out so it initially takes a few hours and make sure your program will fill that time period.

Once you've put the entire program together, offer it to various groups as either an initial lecture or speaking engagement. Once you're about to do your speaking engagement, make sure to have an expanded program available so you can offer it to anyone who becomes interested after your talk. Advise those that you speak to that you are running a full fledged workshop on how to build self-esteem and self-confidence and set the date at least a month off so that anyone who wants to learn more will want to attend your seminar or workshop. Always schedule future events sufficiently in advance that those who want to attend can make their plans to attend.

n. Offer Fear of Flying Anxiety Resolution Courses

Most airlines recognize that fear of flying anxiety is a drawback to their passengers. Every time there is a major crash in America, there is a surge of cancellations as people react to their fears. There are even a few celebrities who are well known for their fear of flying and would rather drive a bus instead of flying. John Madden, the football commentator, is a prime example. Can you imagine if someone like him would undergo hypnosis or Emotional Freedom Technique and eliminate his fear permanently? What would that do for the airlines? It would improve it.

If you have the capacity to assist people in eliminating their fear of flying, then you might want to consider offering them a program to do exactly that. You could offer it to the airlines and suggest that they pay for it or you could suggest that the passengers pay half of it. Either way, if you can deliver the results you'll get a huge following in short order. Fear of flying detracts from the enjoyment of traveling for many passengers. If you could guarantee relief to them, you'd have them coming from every direction to attend your seminar/workshop.

o. Offer Fear of Dentists Anxiety Resolution Courses

Dental pain is a notorious deterrent people to visiting a dentist. Many adults simply don't visit the dentist because of the dental pain they experienced as children which traumatized them to the point they never want to go back. Instead, they wait until their teeth start to hurt, throb, fall out or fall apart and then they go because they're desperate. Even those who do go to a dentist often go less frequently than they should because of their fear of pain. If you can offer dentists a program that will eliminate fear of dentists or a pediatric class that would eliminate fear from children, you'd have a built in practice on that alone.

Dental fear is so great for so many people that there are now dentists who advertise that they'll administer general anesthesia to you in order to work on your entire mouth in one sitting. People undergo general anesthesia which has multiple potentially harmful side effects just to avoid the prospect of some pain at the hands of a dentist working on their mouth and would rather endure the aftereffects of anesthesia than just have a dentist work on them.

Of course, if you could offer a pediatric class, it would be even better because if you could eliminate children's initial fears of dentists, they wouldn't be traumatized in the first place and then their adult fears would be eliminated before they begin.

p.   Teach How to Overcome Car Sickness Classes

Many children and some adults routinely get sick while riding in a car or bus. This can have a very bad effect upon their health and happiness if it happens with any regularity. Consider how every teacher who takes their students on a field trip feels knowing they're going to have to deal with at least a few children who have car sickness problems. If they could eliminate that problem, it would make their trips much better for all involved.

You can initially offer a free course to one class in an elementary school and once you're successful with them and have eliminated all car sickness from its students, you'll find that you'll have a built in audience.

q.   Teach How to Overcome Sea Sickness

Sea sickness can be a big deterrent to taking a cruise for many people. If they know they may get sick while at sea, they often simply won't book their trip. This obviously has an adverse effect upon the cruise industry. While many people take medication to control their sea sickness, many find that it leaves them feeling groggy and disoriented. That's not the way most people want to spend their vacation. However, when they look for another alternative, there never has been one - until now. If you practice EFT you have a perfect technique to eliminate sea sickness almost immediately. One approach could be to offer such a class to travel agencies and they could, in turn, offer them to their prospective passengers who suffer from sea sickness. If you can eliminate their clients sea sickness, you'll find a lot of new business waiting for you.

Another approach is to offer your services to cruise lines on board their ocean liners. That way, if their passengers begin to get sea sick while at sea, they'll have something other than a drug to give them. You may offer to barter with them for free travel along with a reasonable salary for working on their passengers. Or you may consider working on a "Per Passenger" rate so that the more you work, the more you earn. Or you may consider offering to be an independent contractor if the ship is large enough to have enough potential clients to support your efforts on a single trip. And it doesn't hurt to choose trips that experience notoriously rough seas. That way, you're almost certain to have a full schedule of people to work on throughout your trip.

r.   Offer Abundance Workshops

Many people have a lot of resistance to accepting abundance into their lives due to their early training and negative education. They may have heard one or both of their parents tell them things like "Money doesn't grow on trees" or "you have to work hard to get ahead in this life" or any number of alternatives to those self-limiting beliefs. Of course, their parents may have heard those exact words coming from their parents and it changed their lives for the worse as well, but the truth is, none of that way of thinking needs to be continued any longer.

If your particular type of practice includes helping people change how they think about the world, then this is one of the most powerful programs you can offer the public. Most people don't accept that life can be easy or that they are entitled to abundance in their life. Instead, they steadfastly hold onto those outmoded self-limiting beliefs that hold them back from all forms of abundance. If you teach Hypnosis or Emotional Freedom Technique or a host of other types of techniques that address this type of outmoded thinking, this is the perfect workshop for you to offer because you can actually assist them. It will not only help you increase your practice, it will help many people find another way to be in the world that serves them better.

When you offer such a workshop, make sure that you advertise it as not just about money, but about every aspect of the students' lives. Abundance is not just about failing to make enough money, it is about not having enough love, health and lots of other things. It is about not believing you are good enough or worthy of having more than you presently do and not knowing what to do about it. All of these things can be eliminated and resolved by using EFT in the proper fashion and once resolved, they remain changed permanently. This could be the most powerful workshop you could ever teach. It is important that you be very prepared to teach it and know all about the Law of Attraction and how it works as well as how to use EFT to eliminate all the self-limiting beliefs that drive a lack of anything in one's life.

s.   Offer Stress Reduction for Clergy Members

While much of the clergy is charged with helping others cope with the world, who helps the clergy? Most clergy members would say they take solace in the Lord, Jesus, Buddha, Mohammed or Moses, but many times that's still not quite enough to assist them with everyday problems that arise. That causes personal stress and often they don't want to take such stress to their superiors and they're left to cope with it on their own.

If you run stress reduction classes of any sort offer a specific class or workshop to help clergy members - and only clergy members - reduce stress would be a Godsend for them. Inform them that only clergy members will be present so they feel safe and private and they'll know they won't be part of an overall group so they can maintain their image as a clergy member. When you're successful at reducing their stress levels and doing it quickly and effortlessly, you'll not only help them cope better with their lives, you will also insure their referrals of anyone they can't handle in the future. You'll also find you're the receive their thanks which can go a long way in the religious community. If clergy members speak well of you, your practice will almost automatically improve.

BECOME THE EXPERT

87.   Write a Book. Become <u>The</u> Expert in Your Field

To become the apparent expert on your topic of expertise, you must first gather all the information you may need to write a book about that topic. Read as many other books and other sources (such as the Internet) on the subject so you are well informed about all alternatives. Then, once you're satisfied that you know whatever you need (or know where to get it) place everything into an outline that contains chapters that make sense and are organized so the entire book is easy to understand. Then write your book. It doesn't have to be that long to be a book of stature - say, 150 pages and it will be substantial enough to establish you as an expert in your field. However, for it to be important in your field, it is imperative that you limit the topic to a particular niche that few, if any, have written about. That way, when people are looking for that particular niche, they will find your book easily. Once you've written a book, you're now an author and that goes a long way toward being considered an expert in that field.

In the past, getting a book published meant you'd have to contact many publishers and show them an abstract or a few chapters and ask them to take you on and publish your book. If they did, you'd probably make as much as $.50 per book. Almost everything else went to the publishing house.

Today, you can publish your own book on the Internet inexpensively and quickly and look very professional doing it. The price of printing the same sized book cost $3.-4. and sell for $14.95. After deducting half for the retailer, the difference winds up in your pocket rather than the publisher's. However, when you self-publish, the amount you may have to sell your book to a retailer could go even higher. Usually, if a bookstore buys your book to place on their shelf, they'll pay you half the list price unless you place it on consignment and then it could go higher. If you want to place it on Amazon.com, it can cost you 60% of the selling price and you still have to ship it to them at your expense. Nonetheless, you can still have a much better income than by making fifty cents on each book that's sold by a mainstream publisher. Either way you go, you still have to do almost all your own publicity and book signing, etc., to get it sold. Publishers don't do much more than print it and distribute it to their normal retail outlets. You can do much the same all on your own if you choose to aggressively market it.

However, the best way to market your own book is to place it on the Internet and send it to as many book reviewers as you can find and then send it to your email list. Keep your printing editions low, that way you don't wind up with a huge number of books gathering dust in your garage because you found a great price for printing in volume.

Don't forget that once your book is completed, you can also make it into an ebook. An ebook is simply your entire book posted on a particular web site on the internet that allows readers to download it for a price. The benefit of this is they can get it anywhere in the world immediately and you get paid almost immediately. If you do this through your own site, it will take special software to accomplish it or you can do it through an online printer like lulu.com. They will sell your book directly through their site, either a hard copy or an email download and pay you a portion of the entire process monthly or quarterly depending upon how many copies you sell during any particular period. There are a number of on line printers and you can find them by typing in "on line printers" into any search engine to find them.

One thing that many authors often do is sell their ebook cheaper than the hard copy. This is a mistake in my view. A better way to sell ebooks is to actually charge more for them, because those who want them immediately are usually willing to pay a premium. However, to give the purchaser a further incentive to buying that ebook at a higher price, add into the sale a related CD or some other benefit like a free admission to a tele-seminar about the same or similar topic. This will often be just enough to make the sale and establish a long term client for you.

If you don't think you can or want to do the writing yourself, there are websites with listings of freelancers who will research and ghost write your book for a fee. Some will negotiate their fee as long as you give them some recognition that they took part in the writing of the book. You can then get cover designers, interior designers and printing houses who will put it all together for you into a nice package and finalize it for you. You'll be able to get your book done in less than six months if you work at it and get it in print in a month or less after that. At that point you're an author and authors are automatically viewed as experts in the eyes of the public. After all, you're reading this aren't you? What do you think of me already? You've more than likely bought this book because it looked good, sounded interesting and you thought you could use it to help yourself build your practice with the help of my expert suggestions. And you're right. Ask yourself if you thought I was an expert in the field of marketing before you bought this book. If so, then there's the proof for you. If not, then by now, you should have come to an opinion on my expertise and I trust it comes down on the side of being an expert.

My point is, didn't you already consider me something of an expert before you even opened the book and read the first few pages? We've all been educated using books all our lives and we automatically think of authors as knowing more than we do - just as they appeared to us when we were students reading textbooks in school or other books as we grew up. It's a natural expectation that the person writing the book knows more than the reader. And usually it is true.

However, the bottom line is that it helps you be viewed as an expert by the general public and to prospective practice members whenever they see that you've taken the time to write a book. It simply improves your overall image. It even improves your image to other professionals, since they were students too at one time and are just as subject to these beliefs.

To get your book published takes a good deal of effort, but it's worth it in the long run because once it's done, it lasts forever. To get it to the point that its ready for printing is the difficult part, but not <u>the</u> most difficult part. That is the marketing of the book itself. However, if you're simply working to establish yourself as an expert, write the book and don't worry too much about marketing it yet. Once you're written your book, you'll find there are many ways to market it both on the Internet and directly in various bookstores and elsewhere if you really want to spend the time doing it. The primary purpose right now is to write it, just so you can say you've written it. The next section will start to explain some of the ways you can market your book.

88.   Offer to Sign Your Books and Lecture at Bookstores

Now, on to marketing your book. Bookstores are in the business of selling books and anything that helps them sell those books is a benefit to them as well as you. Once you've written a book and have it placed in a bookstore, the best thing you can do for yourself and the store is to offer to do a book signing and a short lecture. Of course, any lecture is abbreviated in terms of time, since they want people in their store to browse and buy books after they've heard you talk. Make sure that whatever you speak about is pertinent to your book. It should also be on a topic that is most likely to draw people to attend. If you get people to your lecture and book signing and they like you or are interested in what you've said, they will buy your book.

In order to get them there, you should first get the bookstore to commit to using their email list and their normal mailing list to advertise your lecture and signing well in advance. You should also commit to using your email list as well, but **<u>never</u>** give them your email list directly or they could copy it into their computer and use it for their own purposes in the future. Always make a deal with them to use your own list and send out an email at least two to three times before your lecture in conjunction with them doing the same thing with their list.

You can also put notices in the local newspapers and they will usually carry them in their notices section if you give them sufficient advance notice.

You may also wish to get the bookstore to take out an advertisement in a local paper or a regional paper advertising your book signing and lecture so that new people will show up. In order to get them to do this, you may have to offer to participate in the cost of some of the advertising so they will be more prone to spending money on the event.

Make it an event. Set your starting time clearly and stick to it. Your ending time is another matter. If there are still people waiting to have their book signed or to talk to you, make certain that you stay and attend to them. They will remember your considerate nature well into the future and that benefits your reputation. All in all, a book signing can be a great thing for you as an author and its simultaneously great for the bookstore. It also gives you an opportunity to give a speech and for your followers to meet you personally.

89.   Give Other Authors Testimonials for Their Books

When other authors write their books, one of the best things they can do to get it sold is to have a testimonial on the front and/or back covers from other authors or a recognized name. Testimonials are one of the best ways to sell a book because when people see a recognizable name, they take it for granted that the named person liked the book written by you and they'll also like the book. However, not everyone knows someone who is famous yet, so they turn to their friends and ask them to endorse their book, which is where you come in.

If someone comes to you and asks for your endorsement and you believe the book is worthy of it, then give it. That way, your name is being seen by everyone who sees that book, even if they don't buy it, they get to see you name in print on a book and that helps make you an expert in people's eyes, even if they don't have any other clue of who you are or what you do. Just having your name under a testimonial represents to them that at the very least the author thought enough of you to include your opinion of their book on one of their covers. That makes you important too. So, if you can, in good faith, give a legitimate testimonial, do it every time.

One thing to remember when giving a testimonial, offer to provide more than one version of your testimonial to the author. That way, the author can choose which one he/she likes best. Or they can ask if you will put parts of each one together to make an even better one for them. That way, they don't have to ask for a rewrite since it gives them options and that makes everything easier for both parties.

It is also the way most important people offer testimonials so they don't have to rewrite them repeatedly.

RADIO AND TELEVISION

90.   Appear on Radio Interviews

Appearing for an interview on radio or television is usually going to reach the widest group of listeners possible. For radio interviews, you can even call it in by telephone so you can do it from home or while you're on the road. However, it is always best to telephone in any interview from a stationary location where you can think and express yourself clearly and effectively and where you're sure that you won't lose your telephone connection in the middle of an important thought or part of the conversation.

Offering to be interviewed on health programs is a great way to get your name out to a broad spectrum of people and give them a fuller understanding of what you are offering to the world. Just like with newspapers and television, every radio show is looking for something of interest to put on the airwaves every day. They have a certain block of time to fill each day and they start working on it months in advance so that everything falls into place on the day of the recording. Of course, some radio is live, but they are usually the exception.

When making an offer to appear on any type of show, you should approach it from a similar perspective as when offering a news release to a newspaper. The basic question is "What's in it for the radio station and their listeners?" If you can successfully answer that simple question when making your submission, you'll never miss an opportunity to be interviewed - as long as the interviewer recognizes what their listeners want to hear.

To do this, first determine what type of show you want to be seen in and whether you believe it will benefit you and your purposes first. If it does benefit you, the next step is to determine what it is that they may want from you. Do you do something interesting that hold their listeners' attention for more than the first three minutes? If not, then amend your offering. If you do, build up the most interesting aspects and offer it in a way that will help the station understand what you're talking about and why they would want to use you on their show.

To get an appearance on a radio show, it will help you to send letters (and tapes, CDs or audio email) out at least a month or two in advance to those radio shows you believe will present you in the best light and will give you the best interview. Don't go on a show just to get on radio. If the show has nothing to do with the type of work you already do, find out the purpose the interviewer has for doing the show and make sure it is consistent with your intentions. Listen to the show to get a feel to see if you like what the show does with various topics to determine if you think you will be comfortable being interviewed by them. If not, don't do it. You'll only be sorry. I've heard a few interviewers talk to alternative health care professionals and instead of showing them in the best light and supporting what they do, they tried to undermine them or make them look like anything but professionals. Don't allow that to happen to you - even if you're already in the middle of the interview. You have as much right to control the interview as the interviewer does. Don't let them push you around or belittle you on the airwaves. If they try, immediately push back at them or walk off the show, but don't let them intimidate you into saying or allowing something to be said that you don't agree with just because you want to be nice or be on that show. You'll be far happier if you set your boundaries clearly and then insist they abide by them and honor you. Remember, they have time to fill and if you threaten to walk off their show, they have nothing else to fill it with, so stand your ground. While this rarely happens during legitimate interviews, it was brought to your attention just so you are well prepared in the event it should ever arise.

Sometimes, you can insist upon editorial evaluation of any interview you give before it goes out to the airwaves. I suggest you request that prerogative or the program will go out to the public without you ever having any chance of editing it. The same holds true with television programming. Insist upon the piece coming out the way its been promoted to you and stick to it. You'll be surprised at just how effective you can be in these interviews and how well they reflect upon you and your abilities if they are properly edited and you play a role in the editing process.

If it all fits and you think it will be a good session for you, go for it full ahead. Write their producer a letter explaining what it is you do, why it would be entertaining (remember, that's the business they're in) and why it would serve a good purpose for the public. Once you get your offering done, make sure to set it aside a day or two and then go back and read it again. If it's not perfect, write it again and again until it is. This could be an important occasion for you so it is important to do it well. There's a vast group listeners out there that are just looking for relief of one sort or another and if they feel comfortable with you as they listen to you, they'll find a way to contact you and call you for an appointment. That's how Dr. Phil became such an icon and while he's not always universally seen as a great therapist, he now has his own show. There's proof that a few interviews can make a great deal of difference to your practice, so it's something to actively promote.

Another way to approach various radio stations is to hire an agent and have them find a way into them for a percentage of any fees paid to you or for a flat fee. Since you are not an actor, you likely won't get paid for such appearances, so you'll have to make independent arrangements with any agent beforehand so that they'll be willing to take you on in the first place. If you're going to hire an agent, ask other speakers beforehand for references and check them out on Google ahead of interviewing them so you'll know who they already represent and how well they've done for them. Don't be afraid of aggressively interviewing any prospective agent since they certainly are going to be interviewing you the entire time. They want to know that you can "deliver the goods" when it comes time to do those interviews so he/she will want to see what you can do in advance. Be prepared to prove yourself with them first. This is normal and they'll want to have some input into your presentation just to insure it will be successful. This is all a good idea if you haven't done these types of interviews before. That way, they can give you some advance advice and critique you afterward so you'll improve with each interview. This is not something that comes easily to everybody, but when it goes well, its invaluable for you and your practice.

91. Prepare Press Release, Photographs, CD and DVD for Your Local Television and Radio Stations

Submit material to your local cable channel for inclusion in their events page and/or their nightly news. If it's a slow day and you look interesting to an editor/producer, you never know where you'll wind up. Of course, if you have something of real merit to offer, then it makes more sense to spend a lot of time to prepare it in a professional fashion so it is more likely to be accepted by the broadcasting or cable station. Again, if you get seen on television or heard on radio, many more people get exposed to you and will usually consider you an expert if that's how you are presented. That's how Dr. Phil first was seen on Ophra's show and now he's got his own show. The same has happened to many others and it can happen to you as well if you want that type of attention and exposure. Of course, just like Dr. Phil, you have to be ready for the negative press you can often get as well if they public or press ultimately doesn't like you or what you do.

92. Offer to Be Interviewed on a Television Show

This is probably the best means to get yourself widely known and accepted by the general public. You can reach the widest audience and get the most exposure by being seen by the largest audience and you'll find them on television. They'll sometimes get to know you better than you want them to know you. It is both the best and worst vehicle for anybody to get well known quickly and completely. That's because it not only shows your best points, it also shows your "warts" rather well at the same time. So if you're going to do a television interview, make sure you know your topic intimately beforehand and have an agreement with the interviewer as to what is going to be discussed.

You can do this by submitting an outline of what you want to talk about and getting it approved by the show's producer in advance.

To get a television interview you do just about the same thing you would do to get a radio interview. First, you send them a packet of information about yourself that makes the producer of the show want to put you on their show. Remember, there are plenty of other people doing the same thing, so what ever it is you send to them should look and sound professional and compelling. It would be best to send them a DVD of a prior television or radio interview so they can evaluate beforehand how well you do during interviews and how you look. Television is a visual arts media, so only send things that make you look your best and sound your best.

You may also wish to retain the services of an agent who knows somebody on the particular show you're trying to get onto get you a better chance then just sending in something "cold" and getting rejected because nobody really took a look at it.

Again, it is best to offer to talk about something that the viewers of that particular type of show regularly watch so they will have an interest in what you have to say. Remember that old golden rule "what's in it for me" always dictates what the producers of any show finally put on their show. If they think their audience will like what you have to offer, then there's a much greater likelihood that they'll use you on their show. If what you have to talk about is controversial or offbeat that will also go a long way toward getting you on their show. Whatever it takes to get on such a show is useful as long as they don't in any way dictate to you what you're going to speak about or if they suddenly take an adversarial turn in the interview. As with radio shows, should that happen, make sure to stand your ground and respond to them in a professional fashion, but always hold your own position.

Before you go on, make sure you've already prepared and practiced your initial statement or initial talking points so you look relaxed and polished. You may even wish to practice in front of a video camera and review the tape afterward just to see how you look and what you sound like ahead of time.

That way, you'll be able to identify anything you would like to modify about your appearance or the impression you project.

Remember when you're being interviewed and a question is asked of you, make sure you end your response with an entree into another pertinent question so the interviewer will look good too. It's always a good idea to help the interviewer whenever you can so they are happy that you were interviewed by them by the end of the show. This will help you be asked onto their show again if they have an opening and the responses they received about you were positive. Nothing succeeds like success and making the interviewer's job easier is always a good idea.

When you appear on a television show, you'll find it will often give you great returns for the time and energy spent preparing and attending the interview. In effect, viewers often feel like you've been in their living room with them and that means they're usually comfortable with you and will invite you back again. If they like you during your interview, they'll like you in the future and that is good for you and your practice.

APPEALING TO YOUR
EXISTING PRACTICE MEMBERS

Once you have attracted clients into your office, the question often arises, how do you retain them and get them to return for services regularly? This is asked by most professional practitioners because generally most people would rather stay away from health care offices. Just going to them carries a negative stigma that you "have to go to the doctor" or something like it.

Here are some specific techniques to transform your practice into more of an internal community that will help it feel more like a family to them. If you can generate that feeling among your clients, you'll be a long way towards building loyalty and trust well beyond simple marketing techniques. These offerings are intended to be a starting point for you to find your own way to increase your following and utilize your existing client list.

93. Use the Term "Practice Members" Instead of Clients

Most alternative practitioners term their clients either "customers, clients or patients" depending upon what area they practice in or what prohibitions are imposed upon them by local or state authorities and codes. However, by using the term "practice members" for your clients, it often leads to more loyalty and a greater sense of community for all involved.

When people are a "member" of your practice, they have a built in vested interest in you and your practice. In effect, it becomes more about them, which is the hallmark of all good marketing. Remember, "What's in it for me?" are the words that all marketing and advertising should satisfy in order to be successful. By using the term"practice members," they take a more active interest in what's happening within "their practice" and they want to take a more active role in what's going on as well. This often leads to more people who are willing to volunteer their time to do mailings to other "practice members" or act as the door keeper at various practice events without being paid a salary.

They also start to think of themselves more as part of your practice, so they look forward to returning to your office weekly or more often. This is especially so if you give them something to do while they're waiting to be treated. They also become part of the "elite" of the practice so that others want to join their ranks and help out too. Huckleberry Finn had a great idea when he "sub-contracted" his fence painting job. You may also find that many "practice members" make great employees once you've seen them work at other things on a voluntary basis.

94.   Offer Block Treatment Discount Pricing

This is a method of offering a discount to clients/patients who pay you in a lump sum "up front" before treatment begins. It goes something like this: If you normally charge $125.00 per hour for your time as a therapist or any other service, you instead offer a package of 10 visits for $1,100.00 or as little as $1000.00 if they pay cash. That way, you get your client to commit to 10 treatments ahead of time and you get paid in a lump sum, so you know you're sure to be paid for your services.

This overcomes a number of resistance points. Your client will be more certain to return the full ten times if they've paid for them ahead of time. One thing that many practitioners are aware of is that many clients, although well intentioned, show up once of twice while they're in physical or emotional pain or discomfort, and then, once their crisis has passed, you don't see them again - until the next time. While that may sound normal and reasonable, the fact of the matter is, most clients would benefit more by being treated beyond crisis treatment so that the underlying issues beneath the pain and discomfort is fully eliminated. That usually takes more time than just one or two visits.

That's why it's best to get them to commit to longer treatment (if it is legitimately called for by their condition) for a longer period. Some might think that this approach can or will be abused by the practitioner, but the very start of treatment is actually the best time to offer a comprehensive treatment program to the client while they are motivated to deal with it.

If the client is willing to commit to the more lengthy approach, then a secondary aspect arises which is a personal decision of each practitioner. It is offered solely in order to be fully complete in the offerings made to the reader and is not intended to suggest anything untoward or illegal. However, if the client is willing to commit to the longer treatment program, then, in order to give them further incentive to do so, you may wish to offer them a further discount for paying cash in a lump sum. As mentioned above, an additional 10% off can often be a strong incentive for a client to commit to a long term treatment plan. One reason for offering such a further discount is to offset the cost of them using a credit card to charge their sessions with you. On your side, it will also give you immediate cash to do things with and meet your own obligations. The primary purpose in all this is to give your clients the very best care possible and usually a longer term of care is most beneficial to them, so whatever incentives you can provide to commit to longer term care is in their best interest.

95.   Irregularly Offer a Free Session to a Random Person

This is a unique program that makes going to a practitioner more fun and exciting for everyone. It is probably best used by those practitioners who have clients coming in on an irregular weekly or monthly basis. By offering a free session once every so often randomly to someone who comes into your office, you'll give clients a further incentive to come back often and more consistently. And it doesn't cost you anything but your time to offer it. You'll be surprised at how many people will make a greater effort to be there regularly when they believe they might win something.

One way to conduct this "give away" is to give each person a number or a ticket with a number on it as they come into your office and then have a drawing once a week, month or quarter using a young member of your practice to choose the ticket. Always require them to fill out their name, address and email address on the back of their entry form. That way, you can also get everyone's email address updated on the back of each ticket stub they drop into the gallon jar or whatever you use to draw from. Make a big show of the entire process and post the number each week or month on your website so your practice members will check your site regularly. That way, they are constantly going to your website to visit it and that will increase your web traffic and improve your search engine standings. Do it and watch your practice members warm to the experience and participate more regularly.

You can also do the entire thing on the Internet and give the free session away to those who regularly check their email coming from you. In fact, you can send out your e-newsletter at a certain time each week and put one practice member's name in it and give them a certain period of time, like a day, to write you back or they lose it. That way, they will be more prone to look at your newsletter and do so within a specified period of time. All of which leads to more traffic for your website.

It is also best to set it up in a fashion that makes the entire process visible to everyone who comes into the office, such as putting everyone's name who comes to your office into a closed top fish bowl on a reception desk so that everyone can tell how good their chances are each week or month. Or by putting it in the newsletter, everyone will know who the winner was that week.

Also, make sure to take a photograph of the winner and post it each time you declare a winner on your website and in your office. This helps your practice members build their interest and excitement for the next drawing and establishes a greater sense of community throughout your practice members.

On the other hand, if your particular practice involves people coming to you for intimate or personal problems, they may not wish to have the photograph posted or even have anyone know they're seeing you at all. However, since this book was written to address many different types of alternative health care practices, this concept may aptly apply to your practice. Use your own discretion in determining if you wish to implement it or not.

96.   Institute a "Bring a Friend" Discount Program

If your group or individual sessions could use a boost, then make an offer to your existing clients that if they bring a friend to a group meeting or recommend you to them, it will result in a discount on their next session. It doesn't matter how much of a discount you offer them, as long as they get the idea that you're appreciative of their recommendation. That way, you get new clients coming into your office and your existing clients can feel good about bringing in one of their friends to get the same great treatment they've been getting.

Be very careful about doing this so it doesn't look like a crass commercialization of a holistic practice. It must be done subtly or it could be misinterpreted by your clients that you're not very successful and you need new clients. That conclusion should be avoided at all costs since it will make you look needy instead of prosperous and wanting to share what you do with more people.

One way to do it is to write a letter to your clients and invite them to bring a friend on a particular day or week to expose others to the profound healing they've discovered with you. That way, they're actually doing their friends a favor. Make sure to schedule it only for certain days of the week or times of day that your practice may not be as busy.

Instead of offering them a direct discount or a reduction in your fee, you may consider offering their friends a discount which will give them a greater degree of incentive to come to you while <u>also</u> giving your existing client an <u>additional</u> discount. If you think this is too much to give away, think again.

Once you establish a firm relationship with a client, they will stay with you for a long, long time. That means that whatever it costs or takes to get them into your office in the first place is minuscule when viewed over the long term. Spend the extra money now and reap the benefits over the years a hundred fold.

97. Conduct Informative Office Lectures About What You Do

Give a short lecture (under an hour) weekly, bi-weekly or monthly about what you do in your practice. It can be a description of the techniques you use, a health benefit you want to share or anything else as long as it is interesting and useful for people to attend. The reason for this is to build the interest of your practice members in what you do and explain to them what you do. It gives you the opportunity to inform them about more than just what they think you do or the surface stuff of your practice. You can actually get into the nuances of your technique with them and tell them more about what they might expect if they stay with the program you have in your practice. It also exposes things to them that they may not yet be aware of and which may apply to them.

This way, you also get to interact with your clients on a one to one basis and answer any questions they may have. Make sure to do it regularly and consistently so that people will know when they can come in to hear your lecture or when they can send friends or family members to listen to you at the same time each week. Remember, whoever shows up is a potential client, so always make them excellent lectures. Once you get these type of office lectures down pat, they go easily and will attract new clients into your practice.

Another thing to consider doing is to offer some refreshments at these meetings. It doesn't have to be anything extraordinary, just something that they can eat during a break or when they first arrive. Nothing brings in people better than a little free food, even if it is only for a short period of time. It also makes those who are already interested in hearing you that much happier to be there.

The most important aspect is to make sure you do them consistently each week and have your staff call various practice members the day before and again on the day of the lecture in order to make sure they show up. The extra phone calls may be an additional burden upon you or your staff, but they will reap rewards when you consistently see people at your lectures. It may be best to focus on just a few different people each week so you're certain to have some participants to listen to you since there's nothing more deflating than nobody showing up.

98. Offer Discounts to Volunteers

By offering special discounts to those "practice members" who volunteer to help you and your staff in various ways, you'll give them greater incentive to volunteer and that insures they will come out again and it attracts more volunteers. One incentive is a reduced price for a period of time or services. Another is to offer free sessions for the most helpful volunteers. By offering services that you don't have to pay for out of your own pocket, other than with your time and attention, you're reinforcing your care of them as well as saving them money and you're also saving a lot on taxes, etc. by effectively bartering service for service. Actually, it's not really bartering because there's no *quid pro quo* (value given for value received) because they are actually volunteers and would do the work for you whether you reward them or not. Nonetheless, offering discounts and free services from time to time is a sound way of offering rewards with no out-of-pocket money being spent.

If you get some volunteers who are exceptionally helpful, then it is time to think of more valuable incentives. Perhaps a dinner for them and their spouse or sweetheart or a Broadway play if they like that sort of thing. Anything that is thoughtful and a little more luxurious will do the trick and show your gratitude. And when you clearly show your gratitude, they will want to reciprocate with even more volunteer work for you. It is almost certainly a win/win situation.

99.   Hold Special Healing Days at Your Office

Offering Special Healing Days at your office gives practice members an opportunity for them to experience a full day of whatever type of healing work you do. This gives them a more complete day to process the work you do, but also gives you an opportunity to expose them to other types of healing that would support your work and deepen their healing process. For instance, when I was counsel to the Network Chiropractic Association (now known as Network Spinal Analysis) and a number of Network Chiropractors, they irregularly held what were known as "Clear Days" which were all day experiences of Network Chiropractic (at that time) together with Reiki healers and the Twelve Stages Of Healing as developed by Dr. Donald Epstein, DC. They also often added a troubadour who sang healing and/or spiritual songs to round out the day. By doing all these things in one day, it often would transport practice members into deeper healing processes than they could get by coming into the chiropractic office weekly. it also allows them to immerse themselves in a healing environment for a full day, which is like having a "spa experience" that many people pay big bucks for a day in a salon. It also allows for what I term a "compound healing" experience, which means by coupling different techniques together it gives a more powerful and profound result than any of them when done alone.

100.   Offer Advanced Courses for Qualified Practice Members

Many of your practice members are so impressed with what you do for them that they would like to learn more about it. If what you practice is the type of technique that can be taught, then consider offering advanced courses in your particular specialty to those that are interested. By doing so, you will not only be teaching them what they want to learn, you will also be "spreading the word" about the wonderful healing modality you use. It will also inure to your benefit because whenever you teach others, you become "their teacher" and the obvious expert in the field as far as they're concerned. That improves your image within the community and increases your overall value to the community and makes you more in demand. All of which will improve your practice.

In order to teach your technique, it's best to offer weekend classes that are reasonably priced and give them more value than they expect to receive. When someone takes your workshop or seminar, give them more than you advertise. If you tell them you're going to teach them to do a certain technique, after you've taught it to them, given them a practice session or two, add a new aspect that only your are aware of so they learn it too. Or give them a CD or DVD at the end of the workshop so they go home with something practical and useful. Always give them more than they expect to receive and they'll be a happy group of students who view you as an excellent teacher. Again, it always helps you and your practice.

101. Hold Special Events for "Practice Members" Only

When you have "practice members" you can hold special events for them at a discount or for free every once in a while. That way, your "practice members" get something special in return for their being part of "their" practice which makes them feel more appreciated and like they've received something special just for being part of the practice. By holding special events for "practice members" only, and defining them as regular attending members or volunteers, you'll give your entire practice membership greater incentive to remain regular in their visits and/or get involved as "practice members" volunteers. They'll also feel more appreciated and more excited to be coming to see you on a regular basis, which, again, gives them greater incentive to stay with you and their practice.

a. Offer a Healing Weekend for Practice Members Only

After you've run a few healing days at your office, consider offering a healing intensive weekend in which you will expand the healing day concept. The purpose of this is to give your practice members a longer period of time to be together exclusively in a healing environment while they experience more "compound healing" than at a healing day. Compound healing is when more than one type of healing professional works on that client consecutively. That way, the client receives the benefit of different techniques and different healers working on them from different points of view and in different ways. This can bring about huge changes in a short period of time.

For this type of experience you will need more than just yourself and your immediate staff to provide services to the practice members since more services will be needed to be offered than would be provided on a single day in order to keep them occupied all weekend. You will want to retain the services of other professionals in similar professions or related occupations so that their services will augment and support what you are offering.

A weekend also provides a way of allowing them to fully immerse themselves for a longer period of time which helps them process your ministrations to them and helps them take more steps forward than they normally would be able to do if they were just getting treatment on a weekly basis and then have to go home and face all the everyday stresses of being at home which tend to reverse the positive effects of your treatment. This way, they get treated and then meditate or do another treatment or technique which allows them time to process the information you've imparted to their body and mind. These can be very powerful weekends that your practice members will look forward to after they've experienced the first one. Even if they haven't yet experienced one, they will get the chance to talk to other practice members who have attended one and hear how wonderful they are and then look forward to attending one themselves.

b.   Offer a Healing Retreat to Practice Members Only

Once you've run a number of healing weekends, you may wish to offer a healing retreat for 4-5 days in a residential setting. There are a number of such settings around the country and world that rent their places out for prolonged periods and have all the facilities to accommodate such a prolonged retreat. On the east coast there is Kripalu and Omega centers in Massachusetts and upstate New York and on the west coast there is Mount Madonna (affiliated with Omega) and a number of others in California. There are also a number of Budhist and Hindu retreat centers that allow other groups to offer residential retreats at their centers without insisting that they have any affiliation with them in any other way. They often offer vegetarian menus and other amenities that will support a healthy alternative lifestyle to all that attend.

While all of these centers have certain religious affiliates or spiritual approaches, none of them seek to impose their beliefs upon any group that runs their retreat at their center. However, the important aspect of these centers is that they uniformly provide beautiful and quiet environments for your participants to enjoy while they're there which contribute to a wonderful overall experience.

One thing to remember if you're considering running such a retreat: you must be able to "deliver the goods" when it comes to content. All of the more lengthy retreats that I've attended (and I've attended a lot of them) are held by people who have amazing abilities of healing or speaking or both. Or they know enough to hire people who have those capacities. If you're going to run a lengthy retreat, it's best to plan it out meticulously and stick to your schedule as closely as possible. Or, for some people and groups, it works well to plan your schedule as closely as possible and then, once you've gotten started, let it go and do whatever arises in the moment. However, that will depend in large measure on what type and size group you have and how much they insist upon knowing what's coming next beforehand. If they're the types that are pretty loose about things, then anything goes. If not, then stay with the schedule. You're best advised to use your own intuition for those type of decisions as the need arises.

With almost all lengthy retreats, it is often best to offer periods of silence and meditation so that those who receive direct work on them will have time to process whatever has happened within the healing periods. This way, individuals will have a better opportunity to utilize whatever advances they're received during the healing work into their lives.

CDs AND DVDs

102.   Record and Release CD's about Specific Topics

Preparing CD's about your work and how to do specific aspects of it will not only improve your public image, it will further establish you as the apparent expert in your field.   This is very important because whenever someone listens to a CD, they automatically conclude that they are listening to the expert in that field.   If you weren't an expert, where would you get the courage or audacity to release a CD about it? Not only that, but once they hear your CD, if they like it, they'll tell others and that will result in more sales for you and more people who consider you an expert.

Whenever you sell a CD, the profit ratio is excellent after you've made the first one. Of course, that means you must first make the initial CD, which takes a fair amount of effort, but once completed, it will make you a handsome profit. It's an excellent way to make a profit and improve your public image simultaneously.

To make a CD is a fairly simple process. First, you're going to need a software program that allows you to record voice and music and put them together on the same CD. Again, you can find such software on Google.com or any of the other search engines by typing in "audio recording software." Many like Audacity.com, NCH.com (Express Burn), Freecountyr.com are freeware which are available without purchasing anything more from the software designer. Their hope is that you'll like their free software so much that you'll then buy their upgrades and spend some money with them. However, from my experience, free software is not that easy for newbies to use without overcoming a major learning curve.

Instead, you may wish to find a software program that is intended for the uninitiated like me who would rather pay a few bucks and be able to use the program quickly and easily. You may want to look at Adobe's programs and see which one appeals to you or find one on Google or Yahoo. Most of the one's you pay for will more than suffice to help you make a recording and put it on a CD.

Once you have your "master" CD done, you'll find it doesn't take much to make copies on your own computer. However, if you intend to sell more than just a few copies, then it would probably be a good idea to purchase a CD duplicator that automatically makes multiple copies without you having to stand over it and manually insert a blank CD all the time. There are a number of them that will automatically run as many as 50-100 copies without having to refill the machine. One model is called the Nexis CD/DVD Auto Inkjet Printer and costs over a thousand dollars new. These type of machine will automatically print a color print on the face of the CD without doing anything more than programming whatever it is you want to place there. There are some that will only print black and white images and then there are the more expensive type that will do full color printing.

There are also some less expensive duplicating machines that will produce as many as seven CDs at the same time. They look like a tower fan and you must manually insert each CD and the master in order to do the process. However, it is less expensive than the newer models that do the entire process automatically. One brand is the Accutowers or AVPro-7, 9 or 11 (the numbers represent the amount of CDs you can copy at once), which vary in features and cost. The more CDs the machine can copy at once, the more it costs. They vary from as few as one to as many as 11 at once. The costs vary at this time from around $200.- 1,500. and you can find them on the internet by typing in "CD tower duplicators" on any decent search engine and you'll find pages of companies selling them. Once you know how to make a CD and make copies of it, making DADS isn't too much harder and you can normally use the same copying equipment to duplicate it as you use with CDs. It will be explained in the next section.

103. Prepare and Release a DVD about Something Specific

This is effectively the same as posting a video on YouTube.com, but instead of giving it away for free, you make it into a DVD and charge for it. Television is an extremely powerful medium and High Definition DADS are the most effective means of getting your image out to the public. If you can give them something on DVD that will help them, without having to visit you all the time for treatments, you will have them writing, calling and emailing you to purchase it.

Again, while it may take a substantial amount of effort to put together your first DVD, its well worth it in the long run because once you have it made, you can make as many copies as you like afterward. How to actually prepare a DVD, with all the lighting, sound and camera work is beyond the scope of this book. However, there are plenty of videographers out there who are more than willing to do all the shooting, editing and formatting for a price. Once you've made the initial recording, it is there forever and you can sell DADS or give them away as part of other promotions you're running and people will love them. They are the ultimate way to communicate other than in person and most people will not tire of them. They remain in demand whenever you shoot them (if they're shot well and have compelling content) and people are happy to buy them because its just like being there with you in person.

The profit margin is usually much better with DADS than with CDs because most people are more willing to pay more for DADS than for CDs and the cost to reproduce them is just about the same. Of course, the initial cost is more for DADS, but in the long run, they are more in demand over time.

OTHER IDEAS AND
SOME "OFF-THE-WALL" TIPS

104.   Become a Member of a Grievance Committee in Your Field

By volunteering to become a member of a professional Grievance and Review committee within your field of endeavor, you have the dubious opportunity to sit in judgment of other members within that same professional community and evaluate whether any charges lodged against them are valid. By taking on this position, you also have the ability to lend your fair mindedness to the proceedings so that nobody gets "railroaded" by the committee. That can set you apart from others in the eyes of many members because they have to come before you if they commit a breach of your professional society's ethics or standards and a committee of this nature must determine if there's any basis to such an allegation. Then it must determine what to do about it if the claim is accurate. It takes a substantial amount of work to investigate such charges of improprieties, but its well worth it since you are doing a valuable service for your professional organization and it also places you in a position of authority within that group. When that happens, it often leads to others viewing you as a member held in the highest esteem which leads them to be impressed with you and your overall expertise. This all leads others to view you as a leader in your profession and hold you in the highest esteem. Of course, on the down side, some of the people you investigate will view you only as an inquisitor who is trying to harm them or cause them problems but they will be in the minority and the majority of professionals will view you in a positive light.

105. Contact Business Schools to Conduct a Stress Reduction Workshop

Business schools are a haven for stress related problems in their students. All students are stressed almost by definition. Some can't cope as well as others. They have classes to attend and tests to take and as they get closer to graduation, they will be preparing to go out into practice on their own or to work for others. All of this results in major stress for most students. Many times students in advanced schooling become stressed just by virtue of having to take more intense examinations. All of this can lead to unbearable stress for many students. Many become too stressed and as a result, they drop out prematurely and never finish school. This is not only bad for the students, its bad for the school because they rely upon students' tuition to operate. Once a student has dropped out, they usually don't return. All of this is a very negative thing for these type of schools, so if they can help to head such stress off ahead of time, they're usually all for it.

That's where you can come in with your abilities to eliminate stress in others. If your type of practice addresses stress in others, than this is exactly the area for you to investigate.

Approach the students' guidance counselors or admissions office and offer to run an introductory stress reduction class for their students for free. Offer a single class that will help them reduce their stress so they can study more effectively or take tests more effectively. Just coping with the heavy class loads and all the reading necessary to graduate is a heavy load for many students. If you can help them reduce that stress level, your introductory class will be a success.

Once you're finished your class, make sure to get every student to give you a student evaluation sheet regarding how they liked your class. If you've done a good job and the school can see the results of what you've done for their students, you'll have an opportunity to run a regular class after that to help even the most stressed out students get better grades and cope with their classes better. Plus, you'll establish yourself as the expert in stress relief so that once those students graduate and if they have a future need of your services during their careers, they'll seek you out or refer you to others who need stress reduction. It's a win/win combination and it will help build your practice.

106. Contact Alternative Health Care "Colleges" or Schools to See If You Can Teach or Train Their Students

Alternative Health Care Colleges or Schools are filled with people who understand and appreciate alternative health care. You can safely assume they are already open to whatever it is you do in your practice and will embrace it if they are given the slightest chance. So, if your particular practice is on the edge of discovery or is basically a new technique, they are the one's who will be most appreciative of what you're doing and will want to learn more about it.

Offer your services to them and offer to teach a class at their school so their students can learn whatever technique you utilize in your practice. Don't worry about them becoming competition for you. By doing this, you confirm that you're the expert and they are the students and whenever they have something they can't treat or don't feel comfortable with, they'll look to you to refer that client to you. What could be better? Also, don't concern yourself with trying to teach them the specifics of how to do your particular technique. Instead, focus on teaching them the practical side of your practice and how it applies to your technique. Students have no knowledge of how to utilize what they learn in schools and whatever practical help you can give them will be greatly appreciated by them as they try to use what they've learned in practice.

107. Obtain Celebrity Testimonials by Offering Free Services

Celebrity testimonials are exceptionally valuable. All you have to do is look at many commercials and billboards to see just how valuable they have become. So if you want to use a celebrity's testimonial, you have to offer them payment of some sort to get it. If you don't yet have enough money to offer them, consider offering free services to them in exchange for their testimonial. If they truly like what you do and want to use your services, then it just may be a perfect fit between you. Once they start using you as their alternative health care expert, its only a short jump to getting them to give you a testimonial. However, even if you have to pay them for their services, they may be valuable enough to convince regular people to attend your workshops or seminars and that could justify such an investment.

108. Leave Text or Video Comments on YouTube.com or any Other Website That Accepts Comments

When you review a video on YouTube.com or any other video site or website, there is usually a place where you can add a comment underneath whatever you've been watching. Sometimes there are even video comments allowed. There are potentially millions of people who access those comments and if you leave a comment along with your contact information at the end of it, you will be able to turn that into additional contacts for you later. This ones' a long shot, but keep in mind anything is possible. By making legitimate comments anywhere and everywhere, your name is being recorded on the Internet for the search engines to find and the more it shows up in diverse places, the more chances it has of being found by someone searching for you.

TESTING YOUR MARKETING TECHNIQUES

While this is not itself a technique or method for marketing, it is actually more important. Every advertisement or marketing technique you use should be tested before it goes out for publication as well as after it has been in the open market for awhile. Testing is a means by which you determine whether your marketing technique is working effectively or not. That way, if you find that it isn't working well, you can modify it so it will work better the next time you publish it. By publishing, I mean however you put it out to the public, whether it's a print ad or an internet ad, the purpose of publishing is to distribute it to your target audience.

As soon as you finish any new marketing text or any other format such as audio, video or computer driven program, you should show it to others in your office. Make sure they like it first. If they don't like it, modify it until they do like it. That's your first threshold. Once you've modified it, bring it right back to them again and again, until they're happy with it.

Then, take your copy out and try it on family members, friends and other business contacts you can trust and have a good working relationship with so they can take a look at it. Again, if they don't like it, modify it until they do.

Most importantly, find out whether they are moved by your copy to actually do something about the product or service you're advertising. If not, then go back and try again. That's the most important aspect of any advertisement - to get the reader, watcher or listener to take action. If they enjoyed your advertisement, but didn't do anything about trying to buy it or use it, then it didn't fulfill its intended purpose. The only purpose of advertising/marketing is to get someone out there to buy your product or make an appointment to see you for treatment - now or in the future. There is no other reason. Testing is a means by which the marketer can hopefully determine in advance whether they're spending their advertising dollars wisely or not. If you're not seeing an increase in sales within a three month period after you've advertised, then your advertisement isn't doing its job effectively.

Testing isn't just done before an advertisement is published. You must constantly observe your advertising to see what works and what doesn't. As you keep an eye on your advertisements and your resultant sales over a period of time you'll be better able to determine if they're successful or not.

One thing to remember is when you modify an advertisement, only change one small thing or a few words at a time. Then watch to see if there's any discernable change in response. That way, you can determine what made the difference in sales. One man had a vacation home to rent in a beautiful redwood forest and the rent was quite reasonable. However, he could not keep it fully occupied. When he decided to change the wording in his ad, he simply changed it from "vacation home" to "a quaint cottage in a redwood forest" and he always had it filled to capacity after that. Just by changing one or two words and the order of the words can make a world of difference.

On the internet search engines, placement can make all the difference in the world. That's why the top three or more returns on every word search are sponsored links. They're at the top of the page, not the bottom, because that's where people searching the net land on the results page. Ad placement is extremely important on the internet and "tag words" are the bread and butter of every search engine and every website on the net. Those "tag words" are the descriptive words used by every web advertiser to attract people looking for them or their product. If the person searching for something uses a particular "tag word" and the advertiser hasn't used that word to describe his/her website or product, the search engine won't return their website on the search. Wording can be exceptionally important in many ways in advertising. Make sure you test all of your metatags with everyone you're reviewing your copy with to make sure that's how they would search for your product on a search engine. When you ask them how they would search for your product, they may come up with many more and different words than you ever imagined and that can make a huge difference to your marketing results.

Testing can be more than just asking what someone thinks of your ad copy. You can also use it to expand the words used in your advertisement or web copy as well as the metatags you use to describe your web pages. Use testing at every stage of your product development as well as all your advertisements. Use testing once you've put out your advertisements. Use testing after your advertisements have been out on the market for awhile and you're not as busy as you expected or wanted. Change the wording and placement of images and/or colors. All of this can and will make a difference to the bottom line of your advertising. Keep testing every time you speak to a new client and ask them how they discovered you. Ask them what it was that attracted them to use your services. Ask them follow-up questions so you can tell exactly who referred them to you or how they found out about you. All of this comes under the heading of testing. Never stop testing. It works well if you do it and then respond to the answers you get. Don't be afraid to test your ad copy or anything concerning your advertisements. You're paying for them. You might as well get the full benefit for what you've paid.

CONCLUSION

Now that you've presumably read all 108 ways to market your practice, it is time to put your new knowledge to use. Don't sit around and contemplate what to do next. Do something. Anything! If you don't like what you've started doing, change course and make another choice to do something else. Always keep moving when you're in your own business and you're certain to succeed.

If you've been following the directions offered throughout the book, you'll have already chosen the methods and techniques you found most appealing and have started using them successfully. For those who haven't yet found success with the methods you've chosen, try new ones until you find the perfect fit for yourself and your practice. There are enough different and diverse ideas in this book to provide everyone with something that will work for them.

Don't limit yourself to just what's in this book. The ideas and suggestions in this book are intended to lead you to think of even more ways to attract people into your practice. There are perhaps hundreds of other methods you can employ to succeed in your practice and I urge you to find every one of them that suits your needs. Of course, you can modify any of the ideas in this book to fit your own particular needs.

Use this book as a guide to help you build your practice, not as something to follow slavishly. If you fail to do something at the precise time you planned, don't get demoralized and think you've failed. Instead, recognize that these are suggestions and guidelines which can be done at any time and get back to work.

Always know you have the ability to make another choice each day and its your choices that will determine your life and your professional success. Never give up on yourself and never quit. You can be a successful professional in any area you choose if you apply yourself and dedicate yourself to accomplishing your goals.

Whatever it is you decide you need to become a successful alternative health care practitioner is exactly right for you. When you discover what it is, embrace it enthusiastically and persist until you find there are more people coming into your office than you can handle. That's when you can either raise your prices or hire additional staff to handle them all, depending upon what you want your practice to be.

No matter what you do, remember you're always going to have to market your practice in one way or another throughout your career. Get used to it now and embrace that premise and everything will go much easier for you throughout your career.

Whenever you find you're stuck in a self-limiting perspective, use EFT to resolve it. EFT will eventually become a mainstay in your own personal healing and you may find you'll want to share it within the context of your practice as well. It is already sweeping the world and its my belief it will one day be a central part of all healing professions.

Good luck with your marketing efforts and don't forget - never give up! Whatever you choose to do, you can achieve it.

APPENDIX
<u>EMOTIONAL FREEDOM TECHNIQUE</u>

This section has been added to help you learn what Emotional Freedom Technique (EFT) is all about and to teach you how to use it effectively. Once you've learned how to use it, you will be able to eliminate whatever emotional issues that are holding you back from success in your career as an alternative health care practitioner. I am a successful EFT practitioner and know how important this technique can be for you in becoming a successful alternative health care practitioner in any alternative health care field. That's why EFT is included in this book, so those who are interested in changing their lives for the better can take advantage of it. I suggest you review the entire Appendix and become fully familiar with EFT before starting to apply it. You may also want to take a look at our web site and study the EFT web page and video so you can learn it fully before starting to use it. The reason for all this preparation is because it works best when you know how to use it and I want you to be successful when you do use it. If you're not sure whether any of the wordings offered in this book apply to you, I suggest you do them anyway. They can't hurt you and they just might help you access parts of you that you didn't know needed to be worked on. I'm sure you'll find they will help you more than you ever imagined.

Emotional Freedom Technique (EFT) is a technique that eliminates blockages within the meridian system. Those blockages are the cause of all negative thoughts, self-limiting beliefs and pain. By using simple tapping with your fingers at various access points primarily around the face, upper body and hands, you can eliminate those blockages and eliminate your negative issues.

Most people haven't heard of meridians, except within the context of acupuncture. EFT uses a simplified form of acupressure which is basically the same as acupuncture without the needles and it works exceptionally well with emotional issues and pain. Here's a brief history of how it came about. Energy meridians were discovered by Eastern doctors in Tibet and China more than 5,000 years ago and are still being widely used today all over Asia. Eastern health care practitioners regularly "re-energize" the body with acupuncture by inserting needles at various access points along their clients' meridians, thereby eradicating all types of physical maladies. The insertion of needles realigns the energy within the meridians and puts the body back into homeostasis or its normal state.

Acupressure is substantially the same as acupuncture, but in EFT we use 5-7 light taps of two fingers at each meridian access point to effect change. These access points are generally at the starting point of each meridian and there is nothing unusual about the appearance of the skin at those points to denote them as an access point. You just have to know where the are and that's why there is a diagram included with this explanation. By tapping on the points, you effectively break whatever blockages exist within the meridians and that improves your emotions. A good metaphor for this method is tapping the top of a straw that has a bit of milk stuck in the middle of it. As you tap the top of the straw, you break the vacuum above where the milk is located and the milk dissipates easily. Once the blockage is broken, the straw is open to carry air or anything else through it again. Similarly, by breaking the blockages in the meridians through tapping, the life force energy (chi) that would normally flow through them begins to flow again and the negative emotion which originally resulted from the blockage is eliminated. In other words, once the blockage is gone, you can go back to feeling good again. Another good metaphor is by eliminating the clouds from the sky you are able to see the Sun shine again. In reality, the Sun never left. The clouds just covered it up for awhile. The same holds true for you. Once you eliminate the blockages within your meridians which caused the negative emotions to dominate you, the normal positive emotions are uncovered and you will feel positive again.

In case you haven't noticed, there's been no mention of any diagnosis or specific treatment used with EFT because there is none. This is important because that means even a layman can do it. Instead of diagnosing each emotional issue so you can tell which specific meridian is blocked so we can tap on it, we simply tap all the meridian access points every time. That way, we tap them all and "can't miss" the one that's blocked and causing the negative emotion or limiting belief to be experienced by you.

In my view, the primary reason for using EFT is to clear away all of the negative and self-limiting beliefs that hold people back from ultimately being present. Presence is a state of mind that allows you to be here now with whatever is here with you. That may sound a bit esoteric, but it is also a profound way of being in the world. When you are present, you are living in the present moment of now and there are no thoughts getting in your way. Being any other way is to be living in the past or the future and that means you're primarily living in the mind rather than in your being. The reason this is important is because when you are in the past or future, that's when your mind becomes engaged and you often start to worry, become anxious or experience any number of other adverse emotions. In fact, when the mind is left up to its own devices, you will often find yourself fixated upon a problem in your life or practice which may appear insoluble. If that happens, you're thinking of the past (and what went wrong before) or the future (worrying about what will happen next time based upon your projections of your past experiences), but you're not in the present moment.

While many great teachers can move into the present moment at will, most people find it difficult to do because they find they can't stop their minds from incessantly thinking. In those instances where people get hung up in their thoughts and can't find their way into being present, they can use EFT to address and eliminate whatever negative thoughts or emotions are holding them back. If they are worried over something, they can tap on the issue by saying, "Even though I'm worried about _____ I love and accept myself nonetheless."

By the way, we say "I love and accept myself anyway" because it helps the two aspects of the mind (conscious and subconscious) to start working together better and initiate the inner healing process. However, if you find you can't say, "I love myself and accept myself," then simply say words to the effect of, "I'm okay for now," or "I'm doing the best I can," etc.

Once you use the tapping technique correctly, the negative emotions should dissipate quickly. That leaves you open to finding ways to solve the problem you were worried about and you can then move on towards emotional freedom from there. This can become a spiritual quest, but it can also simply be used within the context of business to eliminate all negative emotions, blockages or self-limiting beliefs that hold you back from the success you ultimately deserve.

The developer of EFT, Gary Craig, calls those self-limiting beliefs the "writing on your walls." That means we all have preconceived notions about almost everything in our minds similar to the operating software that is installed in your computer. Only in this instance, the "writing" is installed by people during some of your earliest childhood experiences. As children, we were imbued with certain beliefs about the world and ourselves that affect everything we do throughout the rest of our lives. These "writings" can be as simple as "I'm a bad girl" or "I'm a good girl," "life is difficult", "money doesn't grow on trees" to things as complex as "I never get any attention by being good, so I'll get attention by being bad" or "nothing I ever do is ever good enough." There are many, many writings on the inside of the walls of our brains and all of them affect us for better or worse throughout our life. Remember, they're your operating system.

The writing on our walls usually originated with our parents, siblings or relatives, through our experiences as we grew up. You'll never forget the first time you were scared to death by a mystery movie will you? The fear you felt at that early stage of your life left an indelible image of what fear is to you. That's where all of our thoughts about the world reside - in our heads. To us, they're as real as anything can be because our reality comes from our personal interpretation of our experiences.

However, the true reality of the situation is that those negative feelings aren't just in your head. They also reside within your energy field which flow through your energy meridians. Remember, from the perspective of Emotional Freedom Technique, every negative emotion is a result of a blockage in one or more of your energy meridians due to a traumatic episode earlier in your life. And those blockages will often last for life if left unchanged. Sometimes they hang on quite tenaciously and adversely affect us throughout the course of a lifetime.

Another reason I use Emotional Freedom Technique is because it helps eliminate the energy blockages that cause negative "writing on our walls" or the negative emotions that go with them. Many people enter the alternative healing field in the hope of helping others and making a living at it. Then, as they actually start going about setting up their practice, fears and anxieties often arise and they sometimes worry so much they abandon the entire project. That's because the "writing on their walls" held them back. They were imbued with the self-limiting belief somewhere along the line that they weren't good enough, they didn't know enough or they weren't worthy of success. Those nagging fears start to grow within them to the point that even if they want to believe they're good enough, nothing ever goes right for them, so why try in the first place? This type of repeated "writing" on the "walls" of their mind usually results in them becoming stuck, doing nothing and as a result, they fail in their efforts. Now there is something that can be done about it. EFT is the answer.

If you're going to be successful in the alternative healing field, you need to have clarity and integrity of purpose about what you're doing and how you're going to go about it. So, if you have any "withholds", fears or pre-conceived notions about being in this field, now is the time to recognize and neutralize them. To do that, you're being provided with a series of exercises that will help you address your fears and other "writings" using EFT on the various points noted in the following diagram.

The first thing you need to do to be successful at this technique is to identify or recognize the issues that you have "written on your mind's walls." You're going to be given a series of sample issues that have been discovered to be common to many people who are just starting out on a new venture and then you're going to be given a series of questions and suggestions that will help you identify your own special needs in this area so that you'll have a means to work on your own issues.

- **Negative Wording**

Please note that this technique is unique in that the Set-Up and Sequence (tapping) procedures use some of the most negative wordings possible to achieve results. While I recognize that most people recoil from using any negative affirmations because they've been taught that they don't want to say anything negative to their subconscious mind because it might latch onto it and become adversely affected by it, in EFT the exact opposite is true . . . as long as you're tapping at the same time. In fact, I use the most negative affirmations possible because I've discovered that by saying the most negative things possible, I get better overall results with my clients.

I can already hear your mind asking "How can saying negative things to myself help me?" Here's how.

Remember, the basic premise of EFT is that blockages in the meridians cause negative emotions to arise. The reverse is also true. Saying negative things will cause negative emotions to be felt and as a result, the meridians get blocked. So we say the most negative things we can think of in order to bring up those negative emotions completely so our clients can feel them fully. By doing this, we are actually blocking the meridians because the equation goes both ways. That means that if you're not feeling negative, your meridians won't be blocked and if they're not blocked, all the tapping in the world won't make much difference.

We say all the negative words we can muster (including shouting, screaming and cursing - because they bring up one's emotions better than just speaking the words) and by doing so, we block the meridians. We always say "you must feel it to heal it." If you're not feeling those negative emotions fully, then the tapping won't relieve them. The word relieve is important because to relieve somebody of something, they have to be suffering from it in the first place and if you're not feeling any negative feelings, then there's nothing to relieve. That is, unless you can bring up them up again by saying negative words that will bring them back up into your consciousness. That's why we use negative wordings when we do EFT.

While doing the tapping procedure, use the most negative wording you can think of, knowing it will bring up your negative emotions and they will be quickly resolved and eliminated with the EFT tapping procedure. I've also found that if I settle for using only slightly negative wording while tapping, my clients don't get as much relief as they do with the most negative wording.

Don't be concerned that you are using negative statements because they'll actually work better to eliminate your problem than if you used positive statements or positive affirmations. Not only that, once the negative feelings have been eliminated fully, you'll usually find that you feel naturally positive. However, if you still feel so inclined, you can introduce all the positive affirmations you want and fill any void that resulted from the tapping with positive emotions. It is called the "Choices Method" which was introduced by Dr. Patricia Carrington, PhD. and you'll notice some choices have been included in this book to give you an idea of how to use them.

- ### How to Use the Technique

Once you identify the issues you want to deal with, determine your Subjective Understanding Distress Scale, also called SUDS, between 1-10, with 10 being the worst discomfort. SUDS is routinely used in hospital emergency rooms because it recognizes that everyone has different pain thresholds and if you simply use "your own scale," you'll be consistent in your reporting of how well or badly you're feeling as any treatment progresses. In short, it gives you a reference point from which to determine the effectiveness of the later tapping progress on the issue on which you're working.

You begin the technique by using a process called the "Set-Up." This is a procedure (see below for details) where you state the problem and then "accept" yourself at the end of it just as you are, without judgment of what you have been doing to sabotage your goals until now. In reality, you are effectively "speaking" to the subconscious mind. I view this as a "normalization" process between the conscious and subconscious levels of the mind. That way, you start the process in an accepting fashion, telling the subconscious mind that regardless of what it has done "wrong" in your conscious judgment, it is okay, accepted and loved nonetheless.

The tapping and balancing of the energy meridians (called the Sequence) immediately follows (see details below), bringing down the adverse pain or emotional discomfort level progressively as the process continues. The initial Set-Up process also automatically corrects any "psychological reversal" that might be present in your body which could otherwise impair the process of balancing the body's energy. This reversal process is built into the Set-Up and is a way of initially reversing the body's energy system so that the tapping process will work. Don't concern yourself about this since you can't do it wrong using this technique.

The actual EFT process is a progressive series of reductions of the issue (using the SUDS level as a guide), until the issue is brought down to zero. The best way to tell if you are at zero is when you can't focus on the issue or even access it in your mind any longer. Once that happens, the next issue normally arises automatically and makes itself known and the process starts all over again with the new issue. The succeeding rounds may be related, but often are very different from the first issue that arose. Don't be concerned. This is not unusual. This is an ongoing procedure until you have achieved an acceptable level of comfort on all issues that arise during a session. It can be an amazing process, especially if you are persistent at using it on every topic that is disturbing you.

- **The Set-Up**

To do the Set-Up, start by using the tips of two fingers your dominant hand and tapping the meaty side of the opposite hand (called the karate chop point - point 13 KC), while continuously saying words to the effect of, "Even though I have this (fill-in with your own issue) within me, I deeply and completely love and accept myself."

By saying this, you are doing a couple of important things. First, you acknowledge how you feel. Second, you tell the subconscious mind that, although it has an issue (remember, emotions such as anger, fear, sadness, etc. reside in the subconscious) the conscious mind (which is effectively saying the words) "accepts" it and "loves" it. Can you imagine the relief of the subconscious mind, which is only about 3 years of age on an emotional level, hearing that although it's being angry, upset, nervous, sad or afraid to succeed, etc., it is accepted nonetheless by the "mature" conscious side of the mind? That, in and of itself, is a very valuable and profound change of the relationship between the conscious and subconscious parts of the mind. Relief starts almost immediately.

Some people find they can't say they love themselves, usually because they are their own harshest critic and often hate themselves. If this happens, simply say, "Even though I don't feel like I love myself, I accept myself nonetheless" or "I'm okay." This will usually start to resolve that issue immediately.

• **The Sequence**

After doing the Set-Up wording phrases three times, you move on to the Sequence, which consists of tapping the various meridian access points noted on the diagram at the end of this explanation. Repeat a portion of the original Set-Up phraseology (called a Reminder phrase), such as "this issue" or "I'm afraid to succeed," etc., either keeping the words the same or changing them slightly at each meridian access point. This can be as simple as repeating "this issue," or it can be as complex as changing the words substantially with each point and allowing your mind to flow with whatever comes up in that moment (this is called a stream of consciousness). Either way, it works superbly. Remember, getting the words right is important. The subconscious wants to know that you recognize exactly what the issue is before it will allow any relief.

Sometimes an exact description of the issue will not be obvious to you. In situations like this you can say, "Even though I have this issue, I deeply and completely love and accept myself." Rest assured, the subconscious knows what the issue is and will address it. Intention is most important in both instances. This may sound inconsistent with what was just said, but both versions are accurate and true. My best advise is to try the exact words first and if they don't get full relief, move on to the general terms of "this issue" to see what happens. It is often the art of delivery that makes all the difference when using EFT.

Again, people many times object to saying something negative to their subconscious mind fearing that it will seize upon the negative thought and internalize it. As mentioned earlier, that is not the case while doing EFT. This is because you are simultaneously tapping the meridian access points and eliminating the blockages in the meridian that cause the negativity. By doing this, you are neutralizing the negative thought rather than infusing it into the subconscious.

Once you've finished the first round of the Sequence, take a deep breath, close your eyes and evaluate your level of discomfort about the issue you've just worked on. Determine between 1-10 where you are now and if it's less, but not yet a zero or a one, do the Set-up and Sequence again, only this time change the wording slightly to the effect of, "Even though I still have some remaining fear (or whatever it is) about this issue, I deeply and completely love and accept myself," or even "Even though my fear has been somewhat reduced, I still have some more fear about it . . . and I love and accept myself completely." Then tap on all the points again, using Affirmations such as "this remaining fear," etc., until you finish all the points. Again, close your eyes, take a deep breath and determine where you are now on the scale of 1-10. Continue with the Set-ups and Sequences until you get down to a zero or at least a one. I say one because once you're at a one, the meridians will continue to eliminate their energy blockages with the passage of time.

My experience is that sometimes your SUDS number will actually go UP after finishing a Sequence. This can be somewhat disconcerting to the uninitiated because you could become concerned that the technique actually made your condition worse. That is not the case! What's been discovered is that when this happens, the reality is that you actually completely eliminated the first issue immediately and your subconscious moved on to the next most important issue for you automatically! Sometimes, the initial issue was just a cover for the real important issue that carries a higher discomfort level. In order to verify this, close your eyes, take a deep breath and see if you can access the first issue - just as strong as it was when you started. You will usually, if not always, find that you cannot access that issue at all. What has happened is that a different issue or a different aspect of the original issue has popped up unbeknownst to you. That secondary issue can sometimes have a much higher number than the original issue's number. DON'T be concerned by such a turn of events! It is actually a <u>very good</u> thing because you have eliminated the first issue quickly and completely and opened up your subconscious enough to access what the true underlying issue was all along. You then have the opportunity to bring the true issue down to a zero by continuing to tap and get the relief you wanted.

Some people are so surprised by the fact that an issue can be reduced so quickly that they don't believe it and sometimes reject it. This is called a "one minute miracle" because it happens so quickly and completely. You see, the subconscious has no limitations as to how quickly it can change "its mind" like the conscious mind does, so it can change very quickly at times. In fact, much quicker than one might expect or imagine. An issue often changes quickly using EFT because it changes on an energetic basis rather than a logical or cognitive basis. As a result, it often takes no time at all.

If the first issue should be resolved quickly and another one arises that is a different aspect of the original issue, use the closest words to the wording from the old issue to describe the new one. However, if you can't tell what the true nature of the new issue is, you may just say something to the effect of, "Even though this new issue has come up, and I don't know exactly how to describe it, I deeply and completely love and accept myself anyway."

You may then follow up with Affirmations such as "this issue" or "this new issue", "this different aspect", etc. while doing the Sequence. Remember, the subconscious mind always knows what the issue is, even if you can't put exact words to it. It just usually works better with an accurate verbal description.

It is important to note that it is not necessary to tap very hard on each of the access points regardless of how high your SUDS level may be. They will react even with soft to moderate pressure. It is also not necessary to tap more than 5-7 times on each point, except the Nine Gamut point which is continuous. The Meridians are very sensitive and will react with medium pressure if they are placed accurately. That's why it is recommended that you use 5-7 taps using two fingers on your dominant hand, because that way you can't miss the access points.

• **Doing the Full Sequence vs. Short Cut**

The Full Sequence consists of tapping all the points on the head, face, collarbone and underarm together with tapping all the finger nails on the corner points of each nail. The Short Cut uses everything but the finger nails and from my experience, it is just as effective as the Full Sequence if the right wording is used to access the emotions.

To make the entire process even more effective using the Short Cut, you can use both hands to tap both sides of each meridian access point at the same time. While there is no scientific explanation presently known as to why or how this works, my metaphoric explanation is that since the meridians are bilateral in nature (meaning they are the same on both sides of the body) they act like a liquid leveling device (in other words, a long clear hose with colored water in it that seeks its own level over long distances). That means that both sides of meridians strive to remain at an equal level on each side. When one side of the two meridians becomes blocked, the other side then changes its relative energetic position in order to counterbalance the blockage on the other side of the two meridians. Therefore, when you tap on the blocked side and dislodge the blockage, the energy in that meridian frees itself up and starts to flow again. At that point, the energy in the other side of the two meridians starts to flow again and it will continue to flow until it balances itself with the first one again. This is why it sometimes takes a little time for the issue to clear once you've completed the tapping sequence because the energy has to start flowing again and it takes some time.

• The Eye Ladder

On the other hand, if you get the SUDS number down to a 3 or under, there is a simple process that will eliminate the last of the negative charge. It's called the Eye Ladder.

To do the Eye Ladder, tap continuously with two fingers of the dominant hand on the back of the opposite hand between the ring finger and the pinky, in the "valley" part of the hand, the Nine Gamut point (point 14 on the diagram). As you continue to tap, focus your eyes (without moving your head) down towards your feet as far as possible. Then, as if you were climbing a ladder with your eyes, move your eyes upward in six equal steps until your eyes are looking upward as far as possible without lifting your head. (You can also do the same technique by moving your eyes from the top down the same six steps and it is just as effective). Each time you move your eyes, repeat your affirmation words such as "this anger" or "this remaining anger" or "all remaining anger." Continue this process until you are at a zero. That usually only takes one Eye Ladder, but you can do it again if you don't get down to zero the first time. Only use this on a SUDS level 3 or less.

• The Nine Gamut

The Nine Gamut is actually a synthesis of Neuro-Linguistic Programming (NLP) and eye movements in addition to continuous tapping on the back of the hand in the hollow between the pinky finger and the ring finger. This balances the two sides of the brain, the conscious and the subconscious, and is a powerful adjunct to the primary Sequence when a negative issue won't budge.

To do the Nine Gamut technique, continuously tap on the back of the hand between the ring finger bone and the pinky finger bone, in the valley (point 14, Nine Gamut point), while doing the movements directed below.

Without moving the head:
- Look straight forward for 5 taps on the back of the hand
- Close your eyes for 5 taps
- Look down and to the right for 5 taps
- Look down and to the left for 5 taps
- Move your eyes in a clockwise circle starting at 12 o'clock and return to 12 o'clock
- Reverse the movement starting at 12 o'clock and returning to 12 o'clock
- Count 1, 2, 3, 4, 5
- Sing a tune (Happy Birthday works great)
- Count 1, 2, 3, 4, 5

While doing the circular movement, it is helpful to have someone else move their fingers or hand in a clockwise and counterclockwise fashion for you so that your eyes can follow them. It gives your eyes something to focus on while moving. Ask them to watch your eyes closely as you follow their hand.

If the other person notices that your eyes are "jumping around", "skipping" parts of the circle or going straight across sections of the circle, have them move their fingers back and forth across that same section of the circle that was missed while they loudly remind you to concentrate on following the fingers. It has been my experience that when the eyes can follow the circular movement smoothly over that spot they've been skipping, the issue being worked on often vanishes quickly or is reduced dramatically. One way to coach the person is to have the other person repeatedly remind them to "focus " or "concentrate" as they repeatedly move their fingers back and forth over the skip point.

As for why counting to five is done, this is a rote memorization process and therefore, it causes the subject to use the left side/conscious mind to do the counting. Singing a song uses the right side/subconscious mind. By alternating the use of the two sides of the mind, you automatically re-balance them and they work better together.

- **EFT Summary**

The Basic Recipe - Set a SUDS Level of Discomfort from 0-10 before starting

1. The Setup...Repeat 3 times this affirmation:
Say "Even though I have this anger, frustration, fear, etc., I deeply and completely accept myself." while continuously tapping either the Karate Chop point on either hand (for specific issues) or rubbing one of the two Sore Spots (for intense and/or generalized issues).

2. The Sequence...Tap about 5-7 times with two fingers on each of the following energy points found on the attached diagram while repeating the Reminder Phrase at each point.

1	2	3	4	5	6	7	8	9	10	11	12	13
EB	SE	UE	UN	CH	CB	UA	TOH	TH	IF	MF	LF	KC

3. The 9 Gamut Procedure . . .Continuously tap on the Gamut point (9G) (14) while performing each of these 9 actions: (The 9 Gamut is not ordinarily used unless necessary).

(1) Eyes closed (2) Eyes open (3) Eyes hard down right (4) Eyes hard down left (5) Roll eyes in full circle clockwise (6) Roll eyes in circle in other direction (7) Count to 5(8) Hum 2 seconds of a song (9) Count to 5. (Re-evaluate your discomfort level before continuing)

4. The Sequence (again)...Tap between 5-7 times using 2 fingers on each of the energy points while repeating the Reminder Phrase at each point.

Note: In subsequent rounds The Setup affirmation and the Reminder Phrase are adjusted to reflect that you are addressing "this remaining"... (problem) etc. (continue until at a zero).

EFT Tapping Points

Legend:
1 - EB= Eye Brow
2 - SE= Side of Eye
3 - UE= Under Eye
4 - UN= Under Nose
5 - CH= Chin
6 - CB= Collar Bone
7 - UA= Under Arm
8 - TOH= Top of Head
9 - TH= Thumb
10 - Index Finger
11 - Middle Finger
12 - Little Finger
13 - KC=Karate Chop

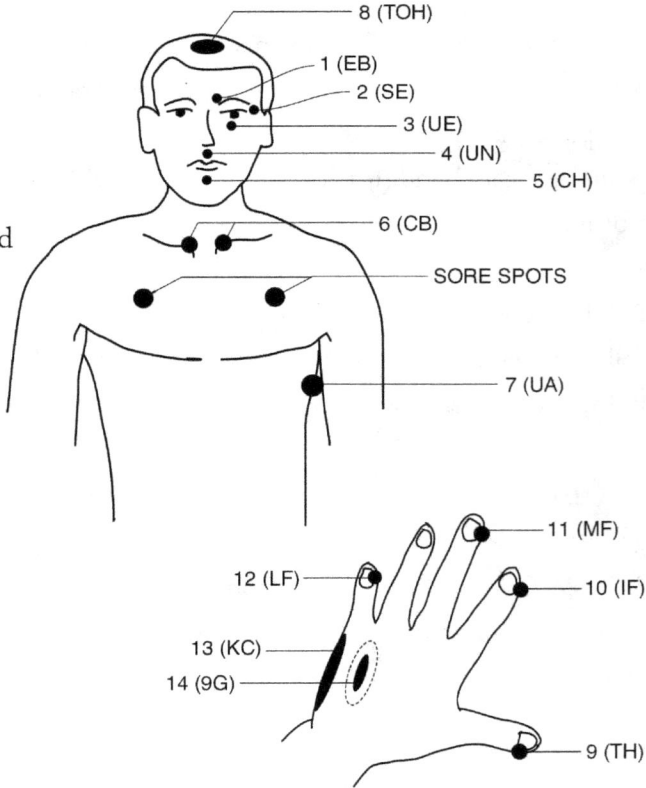

8 (TOH)
1 (EB)
2 (SE)
3 (UE)
4 (UN)
5 (CH)
6 (CB)
SORE SPOTS
7 (UA)

11 (MF)
12 (LF)
10 (IF)
13 (KC)
14 (9G)
9 (TH)

• Using EFT to Balance the Mind

In using EFT to assist you in changing the balance of control between the thinking mind (conscious) and knowing mind (subconscious), we must first acknowledge that we primarily rely upon our thinking mind (which is where our ego resides) to get through life and solve problems. Once we have acknowledged this while using EFT, it can actually lessen the influence the ego mind holds over our life and shift the predominance to the aware or knowing mind which is far more powerful. To change the balance of power from the ego mind to the knowing mind, you may want to use wording like this (remember to use these words as you do the Set-Up and while tapping the side of the palm of your hand):

> "Even though a part of me is thinking and evaluating all the time and I rely upon that part of my mind most of the time to get me through problems, deep within me, I know there is another part of me that really knows the truth at all times, and I love and accept myself for knowing this."

Here's another variation of the above wording that may have a different effect upon you. Again, use this as the wording while doing the Set-Up and tapping the side of the hand:

> "Even though there is a part of my mind that thinks about everything and always wants to be right, always wants to be the one that knows everything and never wants to lose and is always competitive, there is another part of me deep within me that knows that it really doesn't matter who wins or loses and knows it's always safe and that I'm never alone and I love myself for knowing this."

After repeating the Set-Up phrase three times so that the mind really gets the message, you proceed with the Sequence and tap on all of the access points 5-7 times while saying the reminder phrase related to the original words in the Set-Up. They may sound like this for this issue:

"Part of me thinks it knows everything."

"Part of me thinks it's always right or has to be right."

"Part of me thinks it knows everything, but another core part of me actually knows more."

"The part of me that truly knows won't come forward no matter how hard I try to get it to."

"Part of me deep inside knows more than the part of me that thinks it knows. I just can't access that part all the time, but I know it's there."

Change these phrases to make them apply to you as you see fit.

Continue to do rounds of Set-Ups and Sequences until there is no more charge on the issue. The way to tell this is if you try to think about the above issue and find that you just can't access those thoughts any longer. That's when you know you've been successful. Anything less than that and there's more work to do on the topic.

- ## To Address Resistance to Change

The very next issue that everyone appears to have to one extent or another is a "fear of change" or some "resistance to change." We initially address this issue by feeling our emotions within and seeing if we can actually identify a particular "SUDS" number regarding our resistance to change. Again, SUDS means "Subjective Understanding of Distress Scale" and is an effective means of determining the client's subjective level of discomfort or distress level about any particular issue we're interested in resolving. The only reason I do this is so that I can keep track of how far along they are as we work together or how much further they have to go to resolve it completely.

A "zero" SUDS feels like you can't access the original feeling at all anymore, no matter how hard you try. A "ten" SUDS is the most feeling of distress or discomfort you can possibly feel about this issue. It is usually displayed with tears, shaking or some other form of physical disturbance or indication. When you say you feel a "ten" about an issue, it means you can't feel any worse discomfort about it than you already are feeling about it. There is nothing higher than a ten on this scale.

Once you've set your SUDS number, you then have a reference point from which to work from and you can start by saying the following words while continuously tapping the "Karate Chop" side of the hand simultaneously as follows:

> "Even though I may have some resistance to change, I deeply and completely love and accept myself."

> "Even though I have some resistance to change, I deeply and completely love and accept myself."

> "Even though I must not want to change or I would have changed already, I love and accept myself fully and completely."

> "I'm not so sure I really want to change. I'm afraid of what's on the other side of change. Yet, I love and accept myself nonetheless."

"Even though I'm not sure I really want to change what I'm doing and I'm not really sure of what I want to do in the future, I deeply and completely love and accept myself."

"Even though I really don't want to change, I completely love and accept myself."

"Even though I really don't want to change, no matter whether it's good for me or not, I deeply and completely love and accept myself nonetheless."

" I actually know that I don't want to change anything about me and that's all there is, I love and accept myself anyway."

After you've completed saying the phrase three times, you then start the Sequence by tapping the various access points around the eyes and head that are noted in the diagram below, while saying the following:

"Any resistance to change I might have."

"This resistance I may have to change."

"All resistance I have to change."

"I'm actually afraid of change."

"I know I don't want to change no matter what."

"Any and all resistance I have to change."

You may find that one particular phrase may stand out for you and you feel that you really resonate with it more than any other. If that is the case, stay with that phrase and repeat it on all the access points. You also may find that tapping on one spot or another may feel better to you or you may find that you get more relief from tapping that spot. Stay with that spot and continue tapping on it until you get greater relief.

After you've done one full Sequence or more using the above wording, take a deep breath and "check in" with yourself to see if the level of negativity has declined from where it was, stayed the same, or has risen. If it has declined, determine the new level and assign it a lower number between one and ten and start again, using the following words while constantly tapping the Karate Chop spot of the hand. This is called the Set-Up:

"Even though my resistance to change has decreased somewhat (or a lot) I still feel like I have more resistance inside me and I love and accept myself nonetheless."

"Even though I still have some resistance to change left within me, I notice that it's somewhat reduced and I love and accept myself fully and completely."

"Even though some of my resistance to change has dissipated, I feel like I still have some resistance to change left within me and I love and accept myself fully and completely."

Then, do the Sequence by tapping all of the access points to the meridians saying the following words at each point:

"Any remaining resistance to change"

"All remaining resistance to change"

"Any and all resistance to change"

"Any and all resistance to change that remains within me"

"All resistance to change that is left within me" etc.

Again, you can say any or all of these sayings as you move around the various access points and if any one of them feels more satisfactory to you, stay with it for the rest of the points.

Now, stop and again close your eyes, take a deep breath and check your level of discomfort (SUDS) again to see if it has changed. If so, determine what level you're at now. If your level has decreased again, do the same technique that you just finished, using wording that addresses the new reduction. Repeat the process until you are down to zero.

I mentioned above that sometimes your original SUDS number may actually go up after the first round of tapping. If that happens, don't be frightened or worried. It's actually a blessing in disguise. It means that you immediately eliminated the original issue quicker than you thought you would and the very next related issue has popped up for you to work on. You must look within and see what aspect of the original issue was resolved and what aspect may be left over that now needs to be addressed. Reword the new issue and work on it exactly as you did on the first issue. First set your SUDS again, note it and then start your Set-Up wording. Change all your words to be consistent with this new and different aspect of the issue and repeat them three (3) times while tapping the Karate Chop spot constantly again. Then do the Sequence. This description was repeated in order to put it into the context for you.

Once you have resolved any and all resistance to change, there are plenty of other issues that you may want to address to get your mind to the point that you feel capable of entering into this new alternative health care practice you have in mind.

Another topic that seems to arise with almost everyone who has had a difficult time in business or enterprise is the fear of abundance or the lack of abundance in their life.

You should remember, I don't go into the base causes of why you find yourself feeling this way in your life. That is not normally within the parameters of the EFT protocol. I simply and easily address the issue directly by acknowledging what it is and working directly on it. In order to that, you would use words substantially like those that follow.

- **For Issues Regarding Abundance or Lack of Abundance**

First set your level of discomfort about achieving abundance between 0-10 with 10 being the highest level of discomfort. Note the number. Then follow this with a Set-Up procedure by saying the following words while you tap the Karate Chop spot of the opposite hand.

> "Even though I don't feel entitled to full abundance, I love and accept myself fully and completely."

> "Even though I want to start a health care practice, I'm afraid that I'll fail just like I've failed at everything else in my life, yet I love and accept myself just the way I am."

> "Even though I can see myself starting my health care practice, my fears are so great about them that I'm sure I'll fail and that's because I'm not really entitled to any form of abundance, yet I love and accept myself anyway."

Then start the Sequence by starting to tap the access point at the juncture of the nose and the eyebrow (on either eyebrow juncture) while you say the following:

"I'm afraid to start my practice."

"I'm not entitled to abundance in my life."

"I've never succeeded at anything else in my life, why should I start now?"

"I've never succeeded at anything before, what makes me think I can do it now?"

"There are so many problems ahead, I'll never be able to overcome them."

"I can never receive abundance because I'm not entitled to love."

"Abundance is for others, but not for me."

"I'm not worthy of abundance because I'm not worthy of love."

"I'm not worthy of love, so I'm not worthy of abundance either."

"Nobody has ever loved me, so why should I love myself."

"Nobody has ever loved me and nobody ever will."

"Love is for others, not for me."

"It's okay to love others, but I'll never be loved."

"I'll never be loved or be abundant."

"Love and abundance go together and I'll never have either one."

"If I earn more money than my peers from school, I'll feel guilty."

"If I become more successful than anyone else, my ego will become inflated."

"I'm not as good as those other students that went to school with me, so I shouldn't make more money than them in my practice and they're not doing that well yet."

"Making money is not what I'm about."

"I'm all about healing others, not making money, therefore, I don't think about making money within my practice. It will take care of itself."

"I didn't get into this type of practice just to make money, so it's not really that important to me, but on the other hand, I'm not making much money."

"I'm not supposed to make much money because of my religious beliefs. That's for other religions."

"Only those other people think about money all the time, I don't. So, that makes me morally superior. Poorer, but morally superior and God likes me better for it."

"My parents never made much money and they were good people. They always said that anyone who makes a lot of money is no good. Therefore, I don't really want to make much money because it would mean I am no good."

"My parents always said bad things about our neighbors who made more money than us and I never want to be thought of as one of them."

"Even though I've always been taught that making money is difficult and takes hard work, I love and accept myself nonetheless fully and completely."

"Even though I've always been told that money doesn't grow on trees and its not easy to earn a living and I've always blindly accepted that concept, I now realize that it doesn't always have to be difficult and I accept myself nonetheless."

"I now realize that I don't have to suffer in order to be successful and I accept myself nonetheless."

"I don't think I can charge enough for my work to earn a living."

"I'm simply not worth what I'm charging for what I'm doing."

"I can't really prove what I'm doing when I do my healing work and as a result, I don't feel truly entitled to be paid for it."

"I'm not a licensed physician and I don't hold any other license, so I feel like I'm a sham and shouldn't charge any more than the barest minium for what I do."

"I don't have a license for anything that I'm doing, so how can I legitimately charge for it?"

"If anyone discovered how little I really know about healing or anything I'm charging for, they'd string me up and tar and feather me or sue me."

"I don't believe I deserve to be paid for what I do."

"I don't believe I deserve to be paid for what I do, so how can I expect anyone else to believe they should pay me?"

"I don't believe I'm worthy enough to be paid for what I do, so why should anyone else think so?"

"I don't have the courage to charge anyone for what I do."

If you find that you've reduced your SUDS to a 3 or less, use the Eye Ladder saying:

"All remaining resistance to abundance."

Next, move your eyes up one "rung" of the ladder and say the words again,

"All resistance to abundance."

Continue the process, moving your eyes up the next five "rungs" of the ladder saying similar words at each rung. Make sure you continue to tap on the back of the hand where noted the entire time until you get to the sixth "rung" after which you stop. Then, take a deep breath and check in with yourself and determine the level of discomfort you then have on the issue. It will usually be a zero by the time you finish the sixth "rung."

After you've tried all of these wordings using the full sequence, close your eyes, take a deep breath and re-evaluate your SUDS level to see where you're at on the issue of abundance. I hope you noticed that abundance and love were thrown together throughout the wordings. This was done because the two are intimately connected to one another and if you can effect a change in one, the other may well follow and be resolved. This same process of using one emotion to access another is used with many different emotions and the best way to do this is to experiment with them to see which is tied to the other. The same applies to pain tied to emotions.

While EFT is still in its experimental stage, it works exceptionally well in resolving long standing issues that don't want to budge through regular talk therapy, positive affirmations alone and other types of therapies. The best part is that you are able to do it on yourself and take back control of your life. You may find that you will discover new ways that work best for you or your future clients as you go along. I will now show you how to introduce "choices" and positive affirmations into your tapping regimen. You will find them useful in establishing abundance and for infusing a positive spin on resolved issues after you resolve them using the negative affirmations.

- **Choices**

After you've gotten to a zero on the issue of abundance, it's time to introduce positive "choices" and affirmations into your mindset. "Choices" was initially introduced into the work by Patricia Carrington, PhD. from New Jersey who recognized that EFT could be even better if a positive side was introduced after the negative emotions were eliminated.

Some professionals think that it would be best not to leave a void in the psyche so they introduce a positive alternative emotion. This is done by changing the negative verbiage to reflect a more positive outlook on the issue. It sounds like this:

"I now choose to feel abundant at all times and to see abundance in everything and everybody."

"I am abundant beyond my wildest imagination and see abundance of love within me and accept it completely."

"I see myself as abundant and know that the world is filled with love for me and that I am love."

"I am abundant beyond belief and know that I will always be abundant."

"I choose to be fully abundant at all times in the present and future and know that this will last forever if I so choose it."

"I choose abundance now in my life."

"I now choose to recognize that I can be a success easily in my own practice by applying myself to my work and enjoying what I do."

"I now choose to be successful regardless of what challenges come my way."

Another way of addressing this positive affirmation issue is to first eliminate all negative issues and simultaneously introduce positive beliefs about yourself. They would sound like this:

"I now give up the misconception that I am not abundant and that I am unworthy of love and recognize that I am as abundant as I wish to be at all times and worthy of that abundance."

"I now give up the misapprehension that I cannot be abundant and recognize that I am as abundant as I wish to be at all times."

"I choose to give up the misconception that to be successful you have to work long and hard hours and realize that I can be successful naturally and easily."

"I now give up the misunderstanding that I am unlovable and not worthy of abundance and choose to recognize that I am as abundant as I think I am and worthy of being loved and abundant."

This concept was first developed by Rick Moss, PhD. who developed this re-framing technique, called "Pre-Cognitive Re-Education." Re-framing is a technique that displays a particular "writing on one's walls" in a different light than it was originally seen in by the person reading it. Once it is seen by that person in a positive light after giving up the negative belief, the subconscious can then embrace the positive belief easily and completely. Don't be misled by the simplicity of the affirmations, since the subconscious doesn't need complicated techniques to change its basic understanding of the world. In this instance, by combining EFT with this pre-cognitive technique, the subconscious realigns itself integrally and changes quickly and completely.

- ## Procrastination Is Really Fear in Disguise

One final thing to get you motivated to market your practice more than ever before. You've just read through 108 ways to market your practice and it may seem a bit overwhelming. You may already be thinking about watching a movie instead of starting to market your practice. Don't let that happen.

How many times have you found yourself doing just about anything other than what you "have" to do? It happens to all of us more than we like to admit. We usually call this procrastination. <u>I call it fear</u>. Why fear? Because, as I've mentioned before, in my experience most of us have many fears that we don't consciously recognize as such and those fears are really projections of our past recollections of experiences being projected into the future by the workings of our mind.

You see, when you've had a painful or uncomfortable experience, part of you silently says "I'll never let <u>that</u> happen again." The mind then insures that it never happens again by anticipating whenever it could happen and it does whatever it has to in order to keep you safe and comfortable. Unfortunately, whenever your mind has decided that it is not safe for you to be rejected in some fashion or becomes concerned that you might fail at something, it will find just about anything else for you to do other than the very thing you have to do. Hesitation arises and when left unattended, procrastination sets in. The mind basically says that by procrastinating, at least I'm putting off any discomfort you may feel and, who knows, you may even avoid it completely if you wait until the perceived "danger" passes.

In reality, the longer you procrastinate, the worse most situations usually get in life. For example, just think about doing your income taxes. You know you'd rather procrastinate than do them, right? Yet, as April 15th looms ever closer, the pressure mounts until somewhere around April 10th -14th things get so stressful that you feel absolutely forced to do your taxes and you may or may not get them done by the 15th. Many people never get them done on time and then suffer from further anxiety and stress because they have to deal with the consequences of their inaction. It all comes from fear. But remember, you won't have the clients you want in three to six months if you don't start marketing now. It takes awhile for them to respond to your marketing efforts, so you must start now and they will show up later.

Another example is when you go to pick up the phone to make a contact or seek a referral from somebody and suddenly you find something - anything - else to do. It is really the fear of rejection you're feeling and the worry that they may say no. That usually harkens back to when you were young and you asked for something from a parent or somebody else and they said no. That same feeling of rejection and not being welcome that came over you as a child will often come back and the first thing that you want to do is run the other way and avoid that feeling at all costs. So, we wind up going on the Internet looking for email, surfing YouTube, ebay or doing any number of other things to avoid that potential feeling of rejection that we believe is just waiting at the other end as when we pick up the phone and make that call. It is just the fear arising within you.

You already know how can you eliminate the fear so you can lessen your procrastination. Use EFT on it and tap on each of the issues as they arise. The phrases to eliminate fear should sound something like these:

"Even though I can't get started doing what I have to do, I love and accept myself nonetheless."

"Even though I'm afraid of how things are going to turn out, I accept myself anyway."

"I am afraid of rejection and don't want to even start anything as a result, because I'm afraid of how badly things are going to go for me. Yet, I love and accept myself nonetheless."

"I just know I'm going to fail, yet I love and accept myself fully and completely anyway."

"I can't get started at anything because I'm so afraid of how things are going to go for me. Yet, I love and accept myself fully and completely nonetheless."

"I am such a procrastinator because I'm always afraid of rejection. Yet, I love and accept myself fully and completely anyway."

"How can I call people to sell them something when I don't feel comfortable? I'm frightened to death of rejection and I know if I make those calls, I'm going to get rejected. So I just won't make those calls. Yet, I love and accept myself fully and completely nonetheless."

"I'm worried all the time. I feel like such a failure most of the time. Yet I can't tell anyone how I'm feeling and I feel all alone as a result. Yet, somehow I'll muddle through and love myself nonetheless."

"Even though I feel stressed all the time and I am always worried about rejection, I love and accept myself fully and completely."

The idea is to collapse your fears so that you'll feel comfortable approaching new and potential customers and clients. By eliminating your fears and worries, you'll find yourself spending much more time in the present moment instead of in the past or the future thought processes. That way, whenever you're in the present moment, you'll notice there is a lot less to keep you from doing whatever it is you've set out to do. Procrastination will become a thing of the past and you'll feel better about yourself and your purpose in life.

• **Fear of Success as Resistance to Change**

While I've been discussing all of the ways to market your practice, one thing that many people don't realize is that they may have a special resistance lurking behind all the rest of their negative emotions that is less obvious and far more insidious. It's the fear of being too successful. Now most people would say that's ridiculous. They want to be successful and enjoy full abundance of every sort, but the truth is, if they really wanted it on all levels of their being (i.e. conscious, subconscious, unconscious mind), they would have it already. So something is stopping them. I suggest it may be their own fear of success.

When using EFT we call these type of thoughts and beliefs "tail-enders" or a secondary gain. They are self-limiting beliefs that we are not conscious of but which keep us from accomplishing what we think we want to accomplish due to some other negative thought that is stronger than our urge to succeed. It is reminiscent of an automobile accident victim who I once represented who developed a tick that a medical doctor diagnosed as Turrets Syndrome. That diagnosis meant that the "victim" could collect bigger money than he ever thought possible because what was an otherwise innocuous accident had caused him to suffer a noticeable nervous disorder. Nonetheless, as we sat waiting to see the insurance company's doctor together, I mentioned that I could use EFT to help him quickly eliminate the tick. He thought for a moment and then said "Can we wait until after we settle my case?" He was obviously more interested in collecting money than getting out of his immediate discomfort. The collection of more money became a tail-ender or a secondary gain, which, in turn, became more important to that person than their primary purpose which was to eliminate their discomfort.

So, what possible secondary gain or tail-ender could be standing in your way of success? My suggestion is that you stop, put the book down and ask yourself, "What would change in my life if I suddenly became wildly successful?" Wait silently for a few minutes for the answer to come to you and then honor its significance when it becomes clear to you. It could indicate that you'll have to prove yourself every day once you become successful; you may have to work harder than you want to; you may not have any time for your family; you may not be able to put your feet up and watch television or read a book. It could be any number of fears or worries that stop you cold in your tracks instead of supporting your efforts to become successful. But whatever it is, you can easily address and resolve it by using EFT.

One fear that often arises is that of the opinions of others. I had one chiropractor tell me that she held herself back from success because she was concerned if she became too successful too quickly, all of her classmates from school would resent her and despise her. It actually held her back for years before she realized she was the one holding herself back using that as a rationale. This fear often comes as the "Who do you think you are?" disguise, which makes us withdraw from taking the steps we need to succeed and stand within the larger image we truly have available to us when we get out of our own way.

What is the downside to being successful or getting what I want? Take a few minutes with this question, wait and see what answer emerges. You may be surprised. Here's an example. I recently had a person who wanted to succeed in their new chosen field and couldn't understand why things weren't working out for them no matter how hard they tried. After asking the above question, the answer came back that their mother didn't love them and therefore they weren't worthy of success. Sounds strange at first, but it made perfect sense to them and they were able to use EFT to eliminate that self-limiting belief and move through it. Once that was gone, they could work towards their success.

Here are some more sample setups for using EFT to eliminate self-limiting beliefs. If some sound the same or similar to the other ones previously set forth in the book, try them anyway and see if they still carry any charge for you. If they do, then tap on them again until they are fully eliminated.

"Even though I am really afraid to fail at my practice, I love and accept myself anyway."

"Even though I will be humiliated and embarrassed if I fail again, I accept my worries and my fears."

"I've tried before to be successful and it has never worked for me. What makes me think I can do it now? Yet, I love and accept myself fully and completely anyway."

"Even though I am worried that others will think I have an inflated ego and hate me for it if I get too successful, I choose to pursue it anyway."

"Even though there is a part of me that's afraid that if I become successful, I won't have time for a family; to get married; to have a private life; I will be less spiritual; my friends won't like me anymore, I choose to remain strong and confident in my commitment to success."

"I'm actually more afraid of how big I am than how small I am. I'm not sure I could really handle success and everything that comes with it. Yet I choose to move towards success and monitor myself as I go along so that I remain safe at all times."

Of course, as you do all of these Set-Ups, it is important to use parts of them as Reminder Phrases as you do the Sequence and tap all the meridian access points so that whatever issue you've started working on in the Set-Up gets repeated along the way as you tap each point. For instance, if you're working on "I'm really worried that I won't be successful in my new practice", then you'll want to use words during the Sequence that sound like this:

"I'm really worried"
"I fearful I won't be able to do it"
"What if I fail again"
"I'm afraid I'm going to fail again"

"I hate it when I fail"

"I can't take another failure"

"I'm not good enough"

"I'm worried I'm not going to be good enough"

"I'm afraid I can't do it"

By using all these type of words you're reminding the deeper part of you that there is more to this issue than just the simple wording at the beginning. That allows the subconscious mind to fully access the issue and resolve more of it than just the simplistic words at the outset. As you get better at doing this technique, you'll find that the wordings will come to you more naturally and reflect your negative inner feelings which is the whole point of doing it. As you continue to tap on the meridian access points, you eliminate the blockages that cause those negative feelings. That's how the technique works and once all blockages are gone, then there are nothing but positive feelings left within you.

However, if you still don't feel very positive about the issue, you may wish to instill positive affirmations to augment your normal positive feelings.

An example of the wording for "choices" is as follows:

"I now choose to recognize that there is nothing to worry about and I have as much ability to succeed as the most successful professional."

"It is my choice to be successful and I now choose to be a success in my practice."

"I choose to realize that I am just as competent as anyone else and can handle whatever comes my way and be successful at it."

"Despite my previous worries and concerns, I now choose to see myself as competent and capable and know that I will be successful in my new practice."

"It is my choice to be a success."

"I now exercise my choice to be successful in my new practice, knowing I am capable of being successful."

"No matter what else has come before, I now choose to be a competent successful professional with a successful practice."

"I now choose to be a successful professional in a successful practice and nothing can stop me from being a success."

This was offered in order to complete the opportunities for you to eliminate the energetic holds that stop you from succeeding and infusing positive choices for you to be successful. EFT can be a very helpful and powerful tool to bring about change in your life and in your profession. Use it on everything you find standing in your way and before long, you'll find there's nothing left but happiness and success.

Appendix Conclusion

While EFT may look odd and even weird to some people, it is compelling because of one important thing - it works! In fact, it works well for just about everyone with just a little practice. You'll find that as you accurately identify your feelings and recognize your self-limiting beliefs about abundance and success, you'll be able to neutralize those negative thought patterns completely. Don't expect immediate miracles. Instead, persistence is the key to using EFT. Once all of your internal resistance and self-defeating thoughts and emotions are neutralized, success will easily become yours.

If you have any questions about anything in this description, always feel free to contact me by email at ted@tedrobinson.com and I'll respond to you. You can also visit our website anytime for further instructions and explanations at www.centerforinnerhealing.com.

I look forward to hearing from you. Write to us about your successes and I'll include them in our newsletter with your permission.

I trust this new technique will help you on your way to success. As Gary Craig says about it, "Try it on everything." You won't be disappointed. Good luck.

INDEX

QUICK ORDER FORM

Fax Orders:
(516) 248-5354. Send this form.

Telephone Orders:
Call (516) 248-5346. Have your credit card ready.

Postal Orders:
Inner Healing Press, 26 St. Paul's Place, Hempstead, NY 11550

Please send the following:

☐ **How to Open or Improve a Successful Alternative Health Care Practice**
This will help you become a professional in the burgeoning field of alternative health care. It contains marketing information and a host of other information to open your own practice and improve it. (317 pages). $29.95

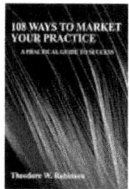

☐ **108 Ways to Market Your Practice**
A practical guide for success. A heavy emphasis on web related marketing techniques and unique ideas on how to jump start a new practice. Topics include Unique Selling Propositions, overcoming procrastination and eliminating resistance to change. An entire appendix teaches Emotional Freedom Technique (EFT) and how to succeed in business. (241 pages). $24.95

Please send me more FREE information on:
☐ Other books   ☐ Speaking/Seminars   ☐ Consulting

Name _____

Address _____

City/State/Zip _____

Telephone _____   Email Address _____

Payment:

☐ **Check**   ☐ **VISA**   ☐ **MasterCard**

Account No. _____   Exp. Date _____

Cardholder's Name _____

Cardholder's Signature _____

Shipping Charges: Continental US: $5. for the first book and $2. for each additional book.

QUICK ORDER FORM

Fax Orders:
(516) 248-5354. Send this form.

Telephone Orders:
Call (516) 248-5346. Have your credit card ready.

Postal Orders:
Inner Healing Press, 26 St. Paul's Place, Hempstead, NY 11550

Please send the following:

☐ **How to Open or Improve a Successful Alternative Health Care Practice**
This will help you become a professional in the burgeoning field of alternative health care. It contains marketing information and a host of other information to open your own practice and improve it. (317 pages). $29.95

☐ **108 Ways to Market Your Practice**
A practical guide for success. A heavy emphasis on web related marketing techniques and unique ideas on how to jump start a new practice. Topics include Unique Selling Propositions, overcoming procrastination and eliminating resistance to change. An entire appendix teaches Emotional Freedom Technique (EFT) and how to succeed in business. (241 pages). $24.95

Please send me more FREE information on:
☐ Other books   ☐ Speaking/Seminars   ☐ Consulting

Name _____

Address _____

City/State/Zip _____

Telephone _____ Email Address _____

Payment:

☐ **Check**   ☐ **VISA**   ☐ **MasterCard**

Account No. _____ Exp. Date _____

Cardholder's Name _____

Cardholder's Signature _____

Shipping Charges: Continental US: $5. for the first book and $2. for each additional book.

www.ingramcontent.com/pod-product-compliance
Lightning Source LLC
Chambersburg PA
CBHW070902270326
41927CB00011B/2436